C-2555 CAREER EXAMINATION SERIES

This is your
PASSBOOK for...

Chief Custodian

Test Preparation Study Guide
Questions & Answers

NLC®

NATIONAL LEARNING CORPORATION®

COPYRIGHT NOTICE

This book is SOLELY intended for, is sold ONLY to, and its use is RESTRICTED to individual, bona fide applicants or candidates who qualify by virtue of having seriously filed applications for appropriate license, certificate, professional and/or promotional advancement, higher school matriculation, scholarship, or other legitimate requirements of education and/or governmental authorities.

This book is NOT intended for use, class instruction, tutoring, training, duplication, copying, reprinting, excerption, or adaptation, etc., by:

1) Other publishers
2) Proprietors and/or Instructors of "Coaching" and/or Preparatory Courses
3) Personnel and/or Training Divisions of commercial, industrial, and governmental organizations
4) Schools, colleges, or universities and/or their departments and staffs, including teachers and other personnel
5) Testing Agencies or Bureaus
6) Study groups which seek by the purchase of a single volume to copy and/or duplicate and/or adapt this material for use by the group as a whole without having purchased individual volumes for each of the members of the group
7) Et al.

Such persons would be in violation of appropriate Federal and State statutes.

PROVISION OF LICENSING AGREEMENTS – Recognized educational, commercial, industrial, and governmental institutions and organizations, and others legitimately engaged in educational pursuits, including training, testing, and measurement activities, may address request for a licensing agreement to the copyright owners, who will determine whether, and under what conditions, including fees and charges, the materials in this book may be used them. In other words, a licensing facility exists for the legitimate use of the material in this book on other than an individual basis. However, it is asseverated and affirmed here that the material in this book CANNOT be used without the receipt of the express permission of such a licensing agreement from the Publishers. Inquiries re licensing should be addressed to the company, attention rights and permissions department.

All rights reserved, including the right of reproduction in whole or in part, in any form or by any means, electronic or mechanical, including photocopying, recording, or by any information storage and retrieval system, without permission in writing from the Publisher.

Copyright © 2024 by
National Learning Corporation

212 Michael Drive, Syosset, NY 11791
(516) 921-8888 • www.passbooks.com
E-mail: info@passbooks.com

PUBLISHED IN THE UNITED STATES OF AMERICA

PASSBOOK® SERIES

THE *PASSBOOK® SERIES* has been created to prepare applicants and candidates for the ultimate academic battlefield – the examination room.

At some time in our lives, each and every one of us may be required to take an examination – for validation, matriculation, admission, qualification, registration, certification, or licensure.

Based on the assumption that every applicant or candidate has met the basic formal educational standards, has taken the required number of courses, and read the necessary texts, the *PASSBOOK® SERIES* furnishes the one special preparation which may assure passing with confidence, instead of failing with insecurity. Examination questions – together with answers – are furnished as the basic vehicle for study so that the mysteries of the examination and its compounding difficulties may be eliminated or diminished by a sure method.

This book is meant to help you pass your examination provided that you qualify and are serious in your objective.

The entire field is reviewed through the huge store of content information which is succinctly presented through a provocative and challenging approach – the question-and-answer method.

A climate of success is established by furnishing the correct answers at the end of each test.

You soon learn to recognize types of questions, forms of questions, and patterns of questioning. You may even begin to anticipate expected outcomes.

You perceive that many questions are repeated or adapted so that you can gain acute insights, which may enable you to score many sure points.

You learn how to confront new questions, or types of questions, and to attack them confidently and work out the correct answers.

You note objectives and emphases, and recognize pitfalls and dangers, so that you may make positive educational adjustments.

Moreover, you are kept fully informed in relation to new concepts, methods, practices, and directions in the field.

You discover that you are actually taking the examination all the time: you are preparing for the examination by "taking" an examination, not by reading extraneous and/or supererogatory textbooks.

In short, this PASSBOOK®, used directedly, should be an important factor in helping you to pass your test.

CHIEF CUSTODIAN

DUTIES

Plans and directs the maintenance, repair and cleaning of a very large school plant or small school district. Supervises a substantial number of semi-skilled or unskilled workers employed on one or more shifts. Oversees the maintenance and repair of building machinery; performs a variety of complex maintenance tasks. Selects and requisitions essential supplies and materials; prepares and submits payrolls and compiles budget estimates. Maintains a variety stock and payroll records and prepares required reports relating to personnel, supplies, and equipment. Work involves more complex and difficult supervisory maintenance and administrative responsibilities than are found in the Head Custodian class due to the greater size and complexity of the school plant or school district which the Chief Custodian is assigned. Supervision is exercised over a substantial number of semi-skilled and unskilled workers employed on one or more shifts in a very large school building. Supervision is exercised over a small number of Head Custodians in a small school district. Work is performed under the supervision of an administrative supervisor, and is reviewed through the inspection of facilities and through reports submitted. Does related work as required.

SCOPE OF THE EXAMINATION

The written test will cover knowledge, skills and/or abilities in such areas as:
1. Principles and practices of building maintenance;
2. Building cleaning;
3. Understanding and interpreting written material;
4. Preparing written material;
5. Supervision; and
6. Administrative supervision.

HOW TO TAKE A TEST

I. YOU MUST PASS AN EXAMINATION

A. *WHAT EVERY CANDIDATE SHOULD KNOW*

Examination applicants often ask us for help in preparing for the written test. What can I study in advance? What kinds of questions will be asked? How will the test be given? How will the papers be graded?

As an applicant for a civil service examination, you may be wondering about some of these things. Our purpose here is to suggest effective methods of advance study and to describe civil service examinations.

Your chances for success on this examination can be increased if you know how to prepare. Those "pre-examination jitters" can be reduced if you know what to expect. You can even experience an adventure in good citizenship if you know why civil service exams are given.

B. *WHY ARE CIVIL SERVICE EXAMINATIONS GIVEN?*

Civil service examinations are important to you in two ways. As a citizen, you want public jobs filled by employees who know how to do their work. As a job seeker, you want a fair chance to compete for that job on an equal footing with other candidates. The best-known means of accomplishing this two-fold goal is the competitive examination.

Exams are widely publicized throughout the nation. They may be administered for jobs in federal, state, city, municipal, town or village governments or agencies.

Any citizen may apply, with some limitations, such as the age or residence of applicants. Your experience and education may be reviewed to see whether you meet the requirements for the particular examination. When these requirements exist, they are reasonable and applied consistently to all applicants. Thus, a competitive examination may cause you some uneasiness now, but it is your privilege and safeguard.

C. *HOW ARE CIVIL SERVICE EXAMS DEVELOPED?*

Examinations are carefully written by trained technicians who are specialists in the field known as "psychological measurement," in consultation with recognized authorities in the field of work that the test will cover. These experts recommend the subject matter areas or skills to be tested; only those knowledges or skills important to your success on the job are included. The most reliable books and source materials available are used as references. Together, the experts and technicians judge the difficulty level of the questions.

Test technicians know how to phrase questions so that the problem is clearly stated. Their ethics do not permit "trick" or "catch" questions. Questions may have been tried out on sample groups, or subjected to statistical analysis, to determine their usefulness.

Written tests are often used in combination with performance tests, ratings of training and experience, and oral interviews. All of these measures combine to form the best-known means of finding the right person for the right job.

II. HOW TO PASS THE WRITTEN TEST

A. NATURE OF THE EXAMINATION

To prepare intelligently for civil service examinations, you should know how they differ from school examinations you have taken. In school you were assigned certain definite pages to read or subjects to cover. The examination questions were quite detailed and usually emphasized memory. Civil service exams, on the other hand, try to discover your present ability to perform the duties of a position, plus your potentiality to learn these duties. In other words, a civil service exam attempts to predict how successful you will be. Questions cover such a broad area that they cannot be as minute and detailed as school exam questions.

In the public service similar kinds of work, or positions, are grouped together in one "class." This process is known as *position-classification*. All the positions in a class are paid according to the salary range for that class. One class title covers all of these positions, and they are all tested by the same examination.

B. FOUR BASIC STEPS

1) Study the announcement

How, then, can you know what subjects to study? Our best answer is: "Learn as much as possible about the class of positions for which you've applied." The exam will test the knowledge, skills and abilities needed to do the work.

Your most valuable source of information about the position you want is the official exam announcement. This announcement lists the training and experience qualifications. Check these standards and apply only if you come reasonably close to meeting them.

The brief description of the position in the examination announcement offers some clues to the subjects which will be tested. Think about the job itself. Review the duties in your mind. Can you perform them, or are there some in which you are rusty? Fill in the blank spots in your preparation.

Many jurisdictions preview the written test in the exam announcement by including a section called "Knowledge and Abilities Required," "Scope of the Examination," or some similar heading. Here you will find out specifically what fields will be tested.

2) Review your own background

Once you learn in general what the position is all about, and what you need to know to do the work, ask yourself which subjects you already know fairly well and which need improvement. You may wonder whether to concentrate on improving your strong areas or on building some background in your fields of weakness. When the announcement has specified "some knowledge" or "considerable knowledge," or has used adjectives like "beginning principles of…" or "advanced … methods," you can get a clue as to the number and difficulty of questions to be asked in any given field. More questions, and hence broader coverage, would be included for those subjects which are more important in the work. Now weigh your strengths and weaknesses against the job requirements and prepare accordingly.

3) Determine the level of the position

Another way to tell how intensively you should prepare is to understand the level of the job for which you are applying. Is it the entering level? In other words, is this the position in which beginners in a field of work are hired? Or is it an intermediate or advanced level? Sometimes this is indicated by such words as "Junior" or "Senior" in the class title. Other jurisdictions use Roman numerals to designate the level – Clerk I, Clerk II, for example. The word "Supervisor" sometimes appears in the title. If the level is not indicated by the title, check the description of duties. Will you be working under very close supervision, or will you have responsibility for independent decisions in this work?

4) Choose appropriate study materials

Now that you know the subjects to be examined and the relative amount of each subject to be covered, you can choose suitable study materials. For beginning level jobs, or even advanced ones, if you have a pronounced weakness in some aspect of your training, read a modern, standard textbook in that field. Be sure it is up to date and has general coverage. Such books are normally available at your library, and the librarian will be glad to help you locate one. For entry-level positions, questions of appropriate difficulty are chosen – neither highly advanced questions, nor those too simple. Such questions require careful thought but not advanced training.

If the position for which you are applying is technical or advanced, you will read more advanced, specialized material. If you are already familiar with the basic principles of your field, elementary textbooks would waste your time. Concentrate on advanced textbooks and technical periodicals. Think through the concepts and review difficult problems in your field.

These are all general sources. You can get more ideas on your own initiative, following these leads. For example, training manuals and publications of the government agency which employs workers in your field can be useful, particularly for technical and professional positions. A letter or visit to the government department involved may result in more specific study suggestions, and certainly will provide you with a more definite idea of the exact nature of the position you are seeking.

III. KINDS OF TESTS

Tests are used for purposes other than measuring knowledge and ability to perform specified duties. For some positions, it is equally important to test ability to make adjustments to new situations or to profit from training. In others, basic mental abilities not dependent on information are essential. Questions which test these things may not appear as pertinent to the duties of the position as those which test for knowledge and information. Yet they are often highly important parts of a fair examination. For very general questions, it is almost impossible to help you direct your study efforts. What we can do is to point out some of the more common of these general abilities needed in public service positions and describe some typical questions.

1) General information

Broad, general information has been found useful for predicting job success in some kinds of work. This is tested in a variety of ways, from vocabulary lists to questions about current events. Basic background in some field of work, such as sociology or economics, may be sampled in a group of questions. Often these are principles which have become familiar to most persons through exposure rather than through formal training. It is difficult to advise you how to study for these questions; being alert to the world around you is our best suggestion.

2) Verbal ability

An example of an ability needed in many positions is verbal or language ability. Verbal ability is, in brief, the ability to use and understand words. Vocabulary and grammar tests are typical measures of this ability. Reading comprehension or paragraph interpretation questions are common in many kinds of civil service tests. You are given a paragraph of written material and asked to find its central meaning.

3) Numerical ability

Number skills can be tested by the familiar arithmetic problem, by checking paired lists of numbers to see which are alike and which are different, or by interpreting charts and graphs. In the latter test, a graph may be printed in the test booklet which you are asked to use as the basis for answering questions.

4) Observation

A popular test for law-enforcement positions is the observation test. A picture is shown to you for several minutes, then taken away. Questions about the picture test your ability to observe both details and larger elements.

5) Following directions

In many positions in the public service, the employee must be able to carry out written instructions dependably and accurately. You may be given a chart with several columns, each column listing a variety of information. The questions require you to carry out directions involving the information given in the chart.

6) Skills and aptitudes

Performance tests effectively measure some manual skills and aptitudes. When the skill is one in which you are trained, such as typing or shorthand, you can practice. These tests are often very much like those given in business school or high school courses. For many of the other skills and aptitudes, however, no short-time preparation can be made. Skills and abilities natural to you or that you have developed throughout your lifetime are being tested.

Many of the general questions just described provide all the data needed to answer the questions and ask you to use your reasoning ability to find the answers. Your best preparation for these tests, as well as for tests of facts and ideas, is to be at your physical and mental best. You, no doubt, have your own methods of getting into an exam-taking mood and keeping "in shape." The next section lists some ideas on this subject.

IV. KINDS OF QUESTIONS

Only rarely is the "essay" question, which you answer in narrative form, used in civil service tests. Civil service tests are usually of the short-answer type. Full instructions for answering these questions will be given to you at the examination. But in case this is your first experience with short-answer questions and separate answer sheets, here is what you need to know:

1) Multiple-choice Questions

Most popular of the short-answer questions is the "multiple choice" or "best answer" question. It can be used, for example, to test for factual knowledge, ability to solve problems or judgment in meeting situations found at work.

A multiple-choice question is normally one of three types—
- It can begin with an incomplete statement followed by several possible endings. You are to find the one ending which *best* completes the statement, although some of the others may not be entirely wrong.
- It can also be a complete statement in the form of a question which is answered by choosing one of the statements listed.

- It can be in the form of a problem – again you select the best answer.

Here is an example of a multiple-choice question with a discussion which should give you some clues as to the method for choosing the right answer:

When an employee has a complaint about his assignment, the action which will *best* help him overcome his difficulty is to
   A. discuss his difficulty with his coworkers
   B. take the problem to the head of the organization
   C. take the problem to the person who gave him the assignment
   D. say nothing to anyone about his complaint

In answering this question, you should study each of the choices to find which is best. Consider choice "A" – Certainly an employee may discuss his complaint with fellow employees, but no change or improvement can result, and the complaint remains unresolved. Choice "B" is a poor choice since the head of the organization probably does not know what assignment you have been given, and taking your problem to him is known as "going over the head" of the supervisor. The supervisor, or person who made the assignment, is the person who can clarify it or correct any injustice. Choice "C" is, therefore, correct. To say nothing, as in choice "D," is unwise. Supervisors have and interest in knowing the problems employees are facing, and the employee is seeking a solution to his problem.

2) True/False Questions

The "true/false" or "right/wrong" form of question is sometimes used. Here a complete statement is given. Your job is to decide whether the statement is right or wrong.

SAMPLE: A roaming cell-phone call to a nearby city costs less than a non-roaming call to a distant city.

This statement is wrong, or false, since roaming calls are more expensive.

This is not a complete list of all possible question forms, although most of the others are variations of these common types. You will always get complete directions for answering questions. Be sure you understand *how* to mark your answers – ask questions until you do.

V. RECORDING YOUR ANSWERS

Computer terminals are used more and more today for many different kinds of exams.

For an examination with very few applicants, you may be told to record your answers in the test booklet itself. Separate answer sheets are much more common. If this separate answer sheet is to be scored by machine – and this is often the case – it is highly important that you mark your answers correctly in order to get credit.

An electronic scoring machine is often used in civil service offices because of the speed with which papers can be scored. Machine-scored answer sheets must be marked with a pencil, which will be given to you. This pencil has a high graphite content which responds to the electronic scoring machine. As a matter of fact, stray dots may register as answers, so do not let your pencil rest on the answer sheet while you are pondering the correct answer. Also, if your pencil lead breaks or is otherwise defective, ask for another.

Since the answer sheet will be dropped in a slot in the scoring machine, be careful not to bend the corners or get the paper crumpled.

The answer sheet normally has five vertical columns of numbers, with 30 numbers to a column. These numbers correspond to the question numbers in your test booklet. After each number, going across the page are four or five pairs of dotted lines. These short dotted lines have small letters or numbers above them. The first two pairs may also have a "T" or "F" above the letters. This indicates that the first two pairs only are to be used if the questions are of the true-false type. If the questions are multiple choice, disregard the "T" and "F" and pay attention only to the small letters or numbers.

Answer your questions in the manner of the sample that follows:

32. The largest city in the United States is
    A. Washington, D.C.
    B. New York City
    C. Chicago
    D. Detroit
    E. San Francisco

1) Choose the answer you think is best. (New York City is the largest, so "B" is correct.)
2) Find the row of dotted lines numbered the same as the question you are answering. (Find row number 32)
3) Find the pair of dotted lines corresponding to the answer. (Find the pair of lines under the mark "B.")
4) Make a solid black mark between the dotted lines.

VI. BEFORE THE TEST

Common sense will help you find procedures to follow to get ready for an examination. Too many of us, however, overlook these sensible measures. Indeed, nervousness and fatigue have been found to be the most serious reasons why applicants fail to do their best on civil service tests. Here is a list of reminders:

- Begin your preparation early – Don't wait until the last minute to go scurrying around for books and materials or to find out what the position is all about.
- Prepare continuously – An hour a night for a week is better than an all-night cram session. This has been definitely established. What is more, a night a week for a month will return better dividends than crowding your study into a shorter period of time.
- Locate the place of the exam – You have been sent a notice telling you when and where to report for the examination. If the location is in a different town or otherwise unfamiliar to you, it would be well to inquire the best route and learn something about the building.
- Relax the night before the test – Allow your mind to rest. Do not study at all that night. Plan some mild recreation or diversion; then go to bed early and get a good night's sleep.
- Get up early enough to make a leisurely trip to the place for the test – This way unforeseen events, traffic snarls, unfamiliar buildings, etc. will not upset you.
- Dress comfortably – A written test is not a fashion show. You will be known by number and not by name, so wear something comfortable.

- Leave excess paraphernalia at home – Shopping bags and odd bundles will get in your way. You need bring only the items mentioned in the official notice you received; usually everything you need is provided. Do not bring reference books to the exam. They will only confuse those last minutes and be taken away from you when in the test room.
- Arrive somewhat ahead of time – If because of transportation schedules you must get there very early, bring a newspaper or magazine to take your mind off yourself while waiting.
- Locate the examination room – When you have found the proper room, you will be directed to the seat or part of the room where you will sit. Sometimes you are given a sheet of instructions to read while you are waiting. Do not fill out any forms until you are told to do so; just read them and be prepared.
- Relax and prepare to listen to the instructions
- If you have any physical problem that may keep you from doing your best, be sure to tell the test administrator. If you are sick or in poor health, you really cannot do your best on the exam. You can come back and take the test some other time.

VII. AT THE TEST

The day of the test is here and you have the test booklet in your hand. The temptation to get going is very strong. Caution! There is more to success than knowing the right answers. You must know how to identify your papers and understand variations in the type of short-answer question used in this particular examination. Follow these suggestions for maximum results from your efforts:

1) Cooperate with the monitor
The test administrator has a duty to create a situation in which you can be as much at ease as possible. He will give instructions, tell you when to begin, check to see that you are marking your answer sheet correctly, and so on. He is not there to guard you, although he will see that your competitors do not take unfair advantage. He wants to help you do your best.

2) Listen to all instructions
Don't jump the gun! Wait until you understand all directions. In most civil service tests you get more time than you need to answer the questions. So don't be in a hurry. Read each word of instructions until you clearly understand the meaning. Study the examples, listen to all announcements and follow directions. Ask questions if you do not understand what to do.

3) Identify your papers
Civil service exams are usually identified by number only. You will be assigned a number; you must not put your name on your test papers. Be sure to copy your number correctly. Since more than one exam may be given, copy your exact examination title.

4) Plan your time
Unless you are told that a test is a "speed" or "rate of work" test, speed itself is usually not important. Time enough to answer all the questions will be provided, but this does not mean that you have all day. An overall time limit has been set. Divide the total time (in minutes) by the number of questions to determine the approximate time you have for each question.

5) Do not linger over difficult questions

If you come across a difficult question, mark it with a paper clip (useful to have along) and come back to it when you have been through the booklet. One caution if you do this – be sure to skip a number on your answer sheet as well. Check often to be sure that you have not lost your place and that you are marking in the row numbered the same as the question you are answering.

6) Read the questions

Be sure you know what the question asks! Many capable people are unsuccessful because they failed to *read* the questions correctly.

7) Answer all questions

Unless you have been instructed that a penalty will be deducted for incorrect answers, it is better to guess than to omit a question.

8) Speed tests

It is often better NOT to guess on speed tests. It has been found that on timed tests people are tempted to spend the last few seconds before time is called in marking answers at random – without even reading them – in the hope of picking up a few extra points. To discourage this practice, the instructions may warn you that your score will be "corrected" for guessing. That is, a penalty will be applied. The incorrect answers will be deducted from the correct ones, or some other penalty formula will be used.

9) Review your answers

If you finish before time is called, go back to the questions you guessed or omitted to give them further thought. Review other answers if you have time.

10) Return your test materials

If you are ready to leave before others have finished or time is called, take ALL your materials to the monitor and leave quietly. Never take any test material with you. The monitor can discover whose papers are not complete, and taking a test booklet may be grounds for disqualification.

VIII. EXAMINATION TECHNIQUES

1) Read the general instructions carefully. These are usually printed on the first page of the exam booklet. As a rule, these instructions refer to the timing of the examination; the fact that you should not start work until the signal and must stop work at a signal, etc. If there are any *special* instructions, such as a choice of questions to be answered, make sure that you note this instruction carefully.

2) When you are ready to start work on the examination, that is as soon as the signal has been given, read the instructions to each question booklet, underline any key words or phrases, such as *least, best, outline, describe* and the like. In this way you will tend to answer as requested rather than discover on reviewing your paper that you *listed without describing*, that you selected the *worst* choice rather than the *best* choice, etc.

3) If the examination is of the objective or multiple-choice type – that is, each question will also give a series of possible answers: A, B, C or D, and you are called upon to select the best answer and write the letter next to that answer on your answer paper – it is advisable to start answering each question in turn. There may be anywhere from 50 to 100 such questions in the three or four hours allotted and you can see how much time would be taken if you read through all the questions before beginning to answer any. Furthermore, if you come across a question or group of questions which you know would be difficult to answer, it would undoubtedly affect your handling of all the other questions.

4) If the examination is of the essay type and contains but a few questions, it is a moot point as to whether you should read all the questions before starting to answer any one. Of course, if you are given a choice – say five out of seven and the like – then it is essential to read all the questions so you can eliminate the two that are most difficult. If, however, you are asked to answer all the questions, there may be danger in trying to answer the easiest one first because you may find that you will spend too much time on it. The best technique is to answer the first question, then proceed to the second, etc.

5) Time your answers. Before the exam begins, write down the time it started, then add the time allowed for the examination and write down the time it must be completed, then divide the time available somewhat as follows:
    - If 3-1/2 hours are allowed, that would be 210 minutes. If you have 80 objective-type questions, that would be an average of 2-1/2 minutes per question. Allow yourself no more than 2 minutes per question, or a total of 160 minutes, which will permit about 50 minutes to review.
    - If for the time allotment of 210 minutes there are 7 essay questions to answer, that would average about 30 minutes a question. Give yourself only 25 minutes per question so that you have about 35 minutes to review.

6) The most important instruction is to *read each question* and make sure you know what is wanted. The second most important instruction is to *time yourself properly* so that you answer every question. The third most important instruction is to *answer every question*. Guess if you have to but include something for each question. Remember that you will receive no credit for a blank and will probably receive some credit if you write something in answer to an essay question. If you guess a letter – say "B" for a multiple-choice question – you may have guessed right. If you leave a blank as an answer to a multiple-choice question, the examiners may respect your feelings but it will not add a point to your score. Some exams may penalize you for wrong answers, so in such cases *only*, you may not want to guess unless you have some basis for your answer.

7) Suggestions
    a. Objective-type questions
        1. Examine the question booklet for proper sequence of pages and questions
        2. Read all instructions carefully
        3. Skip any question which seems too difficult; return to it after all other questions have been answered
        4. Apportion your time properly; do not spend too much time on any single question or group of questions

5. Note and underline key words – *all, most, fewest, least, best, worst, same, opposite,* etc.
6. Pay particular attention to negatives
7. Note unusual option, e.g., unduly long, short, complex, different or similar in content to the body of the question
8. Observe the use of "hedging" words – *probably, may, most likely,* etc.
9. Make sure that your answer is put next to the same number as the question
10. Do not second-guess unless you have good reason to believe the second answer is definitely more correct
11. Cross out original answer if you decide another answer is more accurate; do not erase until you are ready to hand your paper in
12. Answer all questions; guess unless instructed otherwise
13. Leave time for review

   b. Essay questions
   1. Read each question carefully
   2. Determine exactly what is wanted. Underline key words or phrases.
   3. Decide on outline or paragraph answer
   4. Include many different points and elements unless asked to develop any one or two points or elements
   5. Show impartiality by giving pros and cons unless directed to select one side only
   6. Make and write down any assumptions you find necessary to answer the questions
   7. Watch your English, grammar, punctuation and choice of words
   8. Time your answers; don't crowd material

8) Answering the essay question

Most essay questions can be answered by framing the specific response around several key words or ideas. Here are a few such key words or ideas:

M's: manpower, materials, methods, money, management
P's: purpose, program, policy, plan, procedure, practice, problems, pitfalls, personnel, public relations

   a. Six basic steps in handling problems:
   1. Preliminary plan and background development
   2. Collect information, data and facts
   3. Analyze and interpret information, data and facts
   4. Analyze and develop solutions as well as make recommendations
   5. Prepare report and sell recommendations
   6. Install recommendations and follow up effectiveness

   b. Pitfalls to avoid
   1. *Taking things for granted* – A statement of the situation does not necessarily imply that each of the elements is necessarily true; for example, a complaint may be invalid and biased so that all that can be taken for granted is that a complaint has been registered

2. *Considering only one side of a situation* – Wherever possible, indicate several alternatives and then point out the reasons you selected the best one
3. *Failing to indicate follow up* – Whenever your answer indicates action on your part, make certain that you will take proper follow-up action to see how successful your recommendations, procedures or actions turn out to be
4. *Taking too long in answering any single question* – Remember to time your answers properly

IX. AFTER THE TEST

Scoring procedures differ in detail among civil service jurisdictions although the general principles are the same. Whether the papers are hand-scored or graded by machine we have described, they are nearly always graded by number. That is, the person who marks the paper knows only the number – never the name – of the applicant. Not until all the papers have been graded will they be matched with names. If other tests, such as training and experience or oral interview ratings have been given, scores will be combined. Different parts of the examination usually have different weights. For example, the written test might count 60 percent of the final grade, and a rating of training and experience 40 percent. In many jurisdictions, veterans will have a certain number of points added to their grades.

After the final grade has been determined, the names are placed in grade order and an eligible list is established. There are various methods for resolving ties between those who get the same final grade – probably the most common is to place first the name of the person whose application was received first. Job offers are made from the eligible list in the order the names appear on it. You will be notified of your grade and your rank as soon as all these computations have been made. This will be done as rapidly as possible.

People who are found to meet the requirements in the announcement are called "eligibles." Their names are put on a list of eligible candidates. An eligible's chances of getting a job depend on how high he stands on this list and how fast agencies are filling jobs from the list.

When a job is to be filled from a list of eligibles, the agency asks for the names of people on the list of eligibles for that job. When the civil service commission receives this request, it sends to the agency the names of the three people highest on this list. Or, if the job to be filled has specialized requirements, the office sends the agency the names of the top three persons who meet these requirements from the general list.

The appointing officer makes a choice from among the three people whose names were sent to him. If the selected person accepts the appointment, the names of the others are put back on the list to be considered for future openings.

That is the rule in hiring from all kinds of eligible lists, whether they are for typist, carpenter, chemist, or something else. For every vacancy, the appointing officer has his choice of any one of the top three eligibles on the list. This explains why the person whose name is on top of the list sometimes does not get an appointment when some of the persons lower on the list do. If the appointing officer chooses the second or third eligible, the No. 1 eligible does not get a job at once, but stays on the list until he is appointed or the list is terminated.

X. HOW TO PASS THE INTERVIEW TEST

The examination for which you applied requires an oral interview test. You have already taken the written test and you are now being called for the interview test – the final part of the formal examination.

You may think that it is not possible to prepare for an interview test and that there are no procedures to follow during an interview. Our purpose is to point out some things you can do in advance that will help you and some good rules to follow and pitfalls to avoid while you are being interviewed.

What is an interview supposed to test?

The written examination is designed to test the technical knowledge and competence of the candidate; the oral is designed to evaluate intangible qualities, not readily measured otherwise, and to establish a list showing the relative fitness of each candidate – as measured against his competitors – for the position sought. Scoring is not on the basis of "right" and "wrong," but on a sliding scale of values ranging from "not passable" to "outstanding." As a matter of fact, it is possible to achieve a relatively low score without a single "incorrect" answer because of evident weakness in the qualities being measured.

Occasionally, an examination may consist entirely of an oral test – either an individual or a group oral. In such cases, information is sought concerning the technical knowledges and abilities of the candidate, since there has been no written examination for this purpose. More commonly, however, an oral test is used to supplement a written examination.

Who conducts interviews?

The composition of oral boards varies among different jurisdictions. In nearly all, a representative of the personnel department serves as chairman. One of the members of the board may be a representative of the department in which the candidate would work. In some cases, "outside experts" are used, and, frequently, a businessman or some other representative of the general public is asked to serve. Labor and management or other special groups may be represented. The aim is to secure the services of experts in the appropriate field.

However the board is composed, it is a good idea (and not at all improper or unethical) to ascertain in advance of the interview who the members are and what groups they represent. When you are introduced to them, you will have some idea of their backgrounds and interests, and at least you will not stutter and stammer over their names.

What should be done before the interview?

While knowledge about the board members is useful and takes some of the surprise element out of the interview, there is other preparation which is more substantive. It *is* possible to prepare for an oral interview – in several ways:

1) Keep a copy of your application and review it carefully before the interview

This may be the only document before the oral board, and the starting point of the interview. Know what education and experience you have listed there, and the sequence and dates of all of it. Sometimes the board will ask you to review the highlights of your experience for them; you should not have to hem and haw doing it.

2) Study the class specification and the examination announcement

Usually, the oral board has one or both of these to guide them. The qualities, characteristics or knowledges required by the position sought are stated in these documents. They offer valuable clues as to the nature of the oral interview. For example, if the job involves supervisory responsibilities, the announcement will usually indicate that knowledge of modern supervisory methods and the qualifications of the candidate as a supervisor will be tested. If so, you can expect such questions, frequently in the form of a hypothetical situation which you are expected to solve. NEVER go into an oral without knowledge of the duties and responsibilities of the job you seek.

3) Think through each qualification required

Try to visualize the kind of questions you would ask if you were a board member. How well could you answer them? Try especially to appraise your own knowledge and background in each area, *measured against the job sought*, and identify any areas in which you are weak. Be critical and realistic – do not flatter yourself.

4) Do some general reading in areas in which you feel you may be weak

For example, if the job involves supervision and your past experience has NOT, some general reading in supervisory methods and practices, particularly in the field of human relations, might be useful. Do NOT study agency procedures or detailed manuals. The oral board will be testing your understanding and capacity, not your memory.

5) Get a good night's sleep and watch your general health and mental attitude

You will want a clear head at the interview. Take care of a cold or any other minor ailment, and of course, no hangovers.

What should be done on the day of the interview?

Now comes the day of the interview itself. Give yourself plenty of time to get there. Plan to arrive somewhat ahead of the scheduled time, particularly if your appointment is in the fore part of the day. If a previous candidate fails to appear, the board might be ready for you a bit early. By early afternoon an oral board is almost invariably behind schedule if there are many candidates, and you may have to wait. Take along a book or magazine to read, or your application to review, but leave any extraneous material in the waiting room when you go in for your interview. In any event, relax and compose yourself.

The matter of dress is important. The board is forming impressions about you – from your experience, your manners, your attitude, and your appearance. Give your personal appearance careful attention. Dress your best, but not your flashiest. Choose conservative, appropriate clothing, and be sure it is immaculate. This is a business interview, and your appearance should indicate that you regard it as such. Besides, being well groomed and properly dressed will help boost your confidence.

Sooner or later, someone will call your name and escort you into the interview room. *This is it.* From here on you are on your own. It is too late for any more preparation. But remember, you asked for this opportunity to prove your fitness, and you are here because your request was granted.

What happens when you go in?

The usual sequence of events will be as follows: The clerk (who is often the board stenographer) will introduce you to the chairman of the oral board, who will introduce you to the other members of the board. Acknowledge the introductions before you sit down. Do not be surprised if you find a microphone facing you or a stenotypist sitting by. Oral interviews are usually recorded in the event of an appeal or other review.

Usually the chairman of the board will open the interview by reviewing the highlights of your education and work experience from your application – primarily for the benefit of the other members of the board, as well as to get the material into the record. Do not interrupt or comment unless there is an error or significant misinterpretation; if that is the case, do not hesitate. But do not quibble about insignificant matters. Also, he will usually ask you some question about your education, experience or your present job – partly to get you to start talking and to establish the interviewing "rapport." He may start the actual questioning, or turn it over to one of the other members. Frequently, each member undertakes the questioning on a particular area, one in which he is perhaps most competent, so you can expect each member to participate in the examination. Because time is limited, you may also expect some rather abrupt switches in the direction the questioning takes, so do not be upset by it. Normally, a board member will not pursue a single line of questioning unless he discovers a particular strength or weakness.

After each member has participated, the chairman will usually ask whether any member has any further questions, then will ask you if you have anything you wish to add. Unless you are expecting this question, it may floor you. Worse, it may start you off on an extended, extemporaneous speech. The board is not usually seeking more information. The question is principally to offer you a last opportunity to present further qualifications or to indicate that you have nothing to add. So, if you feel that a significant qualification or characteristic has been overlooked, it is proper to point it out in a sentence or so. Do not compliment the board on the thoroughness of their examination – they have been sketchy, and you know it. If you wish, merely say, "No thank you, I have nothing further to add." This is a point where you can "talk yourself out" of a good impression or fail to present an important bit of information. Remember, *you close the interview yourself.*

The chairman will then say, "That is all, Mr. _____, thank you." Do not be startled; the interview is over, and quicker than you think. Thank him, gather your belongings and take your leave. Save your sigh of relief for the other side of the door.

How to put your best foot forward

Throughout this entire process, you may feel that the board individually and collectively is trying to pierce your defenses, seek out your hidden weaknesses and embarrass and confuse you. Actually, this is not true. They are obliged to make an appraisal of your qualifications for the job you are seeking, and they want to see you in your best light. Remember, they must interview all candidates and a non-cooperative candidate may become a failure in spite of their best efforts to bring out his qualifications. Here are 15 suggestions that will help you:

1) Be natural – Keep your attitude confident, not cocky

If you are not confident that you can do the job, do not expect the board to be. Do not apologize for your weaknesses, try to bring out your strong points. The board is interested in a positive, not negative, presentation. Cockiness will antagonize any board member and make him wonder if you are covering up a weakness by a false show of strength.

2) Get comfortable, but don't lounge or sprawl

Sit erectly but not stiffly. A careless posture may lead the board to conclude that you are careless in other things, or at least that you are not impressed by the importance of the occasion. Either conclusion is natural, even if incorrect. Do not fuss with your clothing, a pencil or an ashtray. Your hands may occasionally be useful to emphasize a point; do not let them become a point of distraction.

3) Do not wisecrack or make small talk

This is a serious situation, and your attitude should show that you consider it as such. Further, the time of the board is limited – they do not want to waste it, and neither should you.

4) Do not exaggerate your experience or abilities
In the first place, from information in the application or other interviews and sources, the board may know more about you than you think. Secondly, you probably will not get away with it. An experienced board is rather adept at spotting such a situation, so do not take the chance.

5) If you know a board member, do not make a point of it, yet do not hide it
Certainly you are not fooling him, and probably not the other members of the board. Do not try to take advantage of your acquaintanceship – it will probably do you little good.

6) Do not dominate the interview
Let the board do that. They will give you the clues – do not assume that you have to do all the talking. Realize that the board has a number of questions to ask you, and do not try to take up all the interview time by showing off your extensive knowledge of the answer to the first one.

7) Be attentive
You only have 20 minutes or so, and you should keep your attention at its sharpest throughout. When a member is addressing a problem or question to you, give him your undivided attention. Address your reply principally to him, but do not exclude the other board members.

8) Do not interrupt
A board member may be stating a problem for you to analyze. He will ask you a question when the time comes. Let him state the problem, and wait for the question.

9) Make sure you understand the question
Do not try to answer until you are sure what the question is. If it is not clear, restate it in your own words or ask the board member to clarify it for you. However, do not haggle about minor elements.

10) Reply promptly but not hastily
A common entry on oral board rating sheets is "candidate responded readily," or "candidate hesitated in replies." Respond as promptly and quickly as you can, but do not jump to a hasty, ill-considered answer.

11) Do not be peremptory in your answers
A brief answer is proper – but do not fire your answer back. That is a losing game from your point of view. The board member can probably ask questions much faster than you can answer them.

12) Do not try to create the answer you think the board member wants
He is interested in what kind of mind you have and how it works – not in playing games. Furthermore, he can usually spot this practice and will actually grade you down on it.

13) Do not switch sides in your reply merely to agree with a board member
Frequently, a member will take a contrary position merely to draw you out and to see if you are willing and able to defend your point of view. Do not start a debate, yet do not surrender a good position. If a position is worth taking, it is worth defending.

14) Do not be afraid to admit an error in judgment if you are shown to be wrong

The board knows that you are forced to reply without any opportunity for careful consideration. Your answer may be demonstrably wrong. If so, admit it and get on with the interview.

15) Do not dwell at length on your present job

The opening question may relate to your present assignment. Answer the question but do not go into an extended discussion. You are being examined for a *new* job, not your present one. As a matter of fact, try to phrase ALL your answers in terms of the job for which you are being examined.

Basis of Rating

Probably you will forget most of these "do's" and "don'ts" when you walk into the oral interview room. Even remembering them all will not ensure you a passing grade. Perhaps you did not have the qualifications in the first place. But remembering them will help you to put your best foot forward, without treading on the toes of the board members.

Rumor and popular opinion to the contrary notwithstanding, an oral board wants you to make the best appearance possible. They know you are under pressure – but they also want to see how you respond to it as a guide to what your reaction would be under the pressures of the job you seek. They will be influenced by the degree of poise you display, the personal traits you show and the manner in which you respond.

ABOUT THIS BOOK

This book contains tests divided into Examination Sections. Go through each test, answering every question in the margin. We have also attached a sample answer sheet at the back of the book that can be removed and used. At the end of each test look at the answer key and check your answers. On the ones you got wrong, look at the right answer choice and learn. Do not fill in the answers first. Do not memorize the questions and answers, but understand the answer and principles involved. On your test, the questions will likely be different from the samples. Questions are changed and new ones added. If you understand these past questions you should have success with any changes that arise. Tests may consist of several types of questions. We have additional books on each subject should more study be advisable or necessary for you. Finally, the more you study, the better prepared you will be. This book is intended to be the last thing you study before you walk into the examination room. Prior study of relevant texts is also recommended. NLC publishes some of these in our Fundamental Series. Knowledge and good sense are important factors in passing your exam. Good luck also helps. So now study this Passbook, absorb the material contained within and take that knowledge into the examination. Then do your best to pass that exam.

EXAMINATION SECTION

EXAMINATION SECTION
TEST 1

DIRECTIONS: Each question or incomplete statement is followed by several suggested answers or completions. Select the one that BEST answers the question or completes the statement. *PRINT THE LETTER OF THE CORRECT ANSWER IN THE SPACE AT THE RIGHT.*

1. The KEY figure in any custodial safety program is the 1.____
   A. custodian B. cleaner C. mayor D. commissioner

2. A custodian must inspect or have a maintenance man inspect every window cleaner's safety belt AT LEAST 2.____
   A. each time the windows are washed
   B. once a month
   C. once a year
   D. once every second year

3. A custodian's written instruction to his staff on the subject of security in public buildings should include instructions to 3.____
   A. exclude the public at all times
   B. admit the public at all times
   C. admit the public only if they are neat and well-dressed
   D. admit the public during specified hours

4. A custodian in charge of a building who is normally on duty during the daytime hours in a building which is cleaned at night should 4.____
   A. never make night inspections since he is not responsible for the cleanliness of the building
   B. make night inspections at least once a year
   C. never make night inspections because the cleaners will think he is spying on them
   D. make night inspections at least twice a month

5. The employee MOST likely to find the nests and runways in a building of roaches and vermin is a 5.____
   A. maintenance man B. building custodian
   C. night cleaner D. stationary fireman

6. When mopping, the pails containing the cleaning solutions should be 6.____
   A. slid along the floor to avoid injury due to lifting
   B. kept off the floor, preferably on a rolling platform
   C. shifted from place to place using a mop
   D. equipped with a spigot for applying the mopping solution

7. Of the following, the item that is considered a concrete floor sealer is
   A. water wax
   B. sodium hypochlorite
   C. sodium silicate
   D. linseed oil

8. A material COMMONLY used in detergent is
   A. rock salt
   B. Glauber's salt
   C. tri-sodium phosphate
   D. monosodium glutamate

9. A disinfectant material is one that will
   A. kill germs
   B. dissolve soil and stop odors
   C. give a clean odor and cover a disagreeable odor
   D. prevent soil buildup

10. When scrubbing a wooden floor, it is ADVISABLE to
    A. flood the surface with the cleaning solution in order to float the soil out of all crevices
    B. hose off the loosened soil before starting the scrubbing operation
    C. pick up the used solution as soon as possible
    D. mix a mild acid with the cleaning solution in order to clean the surface quickly

11. Before starting a wall washing operation, it is BEST to
    A. check the temperature of the water
    B. soak the sponge to be used
    C. check the pH of the mixed cleaning solution
    D. dust the wall to be washed

12. Of the following, the MOST nearly correct statement regarding the economical operation of the heating system in a building is that
    A. the heat should always be shut down at 4 P.M. and turned on at 8 A.M.
    B. the heat should be shut down only over the weekend
    C. it is best to keep the heat on at all times so that the number of complaints are kept to a minimum
    D. the times at which the heat is shut down and turned on should be varied depending on the prevailing outdoor temperature

13. A floor made of marble or granite chis imbedded in cement is USUALLY called
    A. terrazzo   B. linoleum   C. palmetto   D. parquet

14. In a 4-wire, 3-phase electrical supply system, the voltage between one phase and ground used for the lighting is MOST NEARLY
    A. 440   B. 230   C. 208   D. 115

15. Of the following, the one that takes the place of a fuse in an electrical circuit is a
    A. transformer
    B. circuit breaker
    C. condenser
    D. knife switch

16. Gas bills are USUALLY computed on the basis of
    A. cubic feet   B. gallons   C. pounds   D. kilowatts

17. An operating oil-fired steam boiler explosion may sometimes be caused by
    A. carrying too high a water level in the boiler
    B. inadequate purging of combustion chamber between fires
    C. overfiring the boiler
    D. carrying too high an oil temperature

18. The one of the following commercial sizes of anthracite which is the LARGEST in size is
    A. stove   B. chestnut   C. pea   D. rice

19. Assume that six windows of a public building facing one street have been consistently broken by boys playing ball after hours and over weekends.
    The BEST solution to this problem is to
    A. post a no ball playing sign on the wall
    B. erect protective screening outside the six windows
    C. post a guard on weekend patrol duty
    D. request special weekend police protection for the property

20. The BEST method or tool to use for cleaning dust from an unplastered cinder-block wall is
    A. a Tampico brush with stock cleaning solution
    B. a vacuum cleaner
    C. water under pressure from hose and nozzle
    D. a feather duster

21. Of the following, the LARGEST individual item of expense in operating a public building is generally the cost of
    A. cleaning   B. heating fuel
    C. electricity   D. elevator service

22. The CHIEF purpose for changing the handle of a floor brush from one side of the brush block to the other side is to
    A. allow the janitor to change hands
    B. make both sides of the brush equally dirty
    C. give both sides of the brush equal wear
    D. change the angle of sweeping

23. Of the following, the weight of mop MOST likely used in the nightly mopping of corridors, halls, or lobbies is _____ ounce.
    A. 8   B. 16   C. 24   D. 50

24. After sweeping assignment is completed, floor brushes should be stored
    A. in a pan of water
    B. by hanging the brushes on pegs or nails
    C. by piling the brushes on each other carefully
    D. in a normal sweeping position, bristles resting on the floor

4 (#1)

25. Nylon-treated scrubbing discs
    A. require more water than scrubbing brushes
    B. require more detergent solution than scrubbing brushes
    C. must be used with cold water only
    D. are generally more effective than steel wool pads

26. Of the following, the BEST material to use to clean exterior bronze is
    A. pumice
    B. paste wax
    C. wire wheel on portable buffer
    D. lemon oil polish

27. The use of trisodium phosphate in cleaning polished marble should be AVOIDED because it
    A. may cause spalling
    B. discolors the surface of the marble
    C. builds up a slick surface on the marble
    D. pits the glazed surface and bleaches the marble

28. The floor area, in square feet, on which a properly treated dustless sweeping cloth can be used before the cloth must be washed is
    A. 500-1000   B. 2000-3000   C. 4000-6000   D. 8000-10000

29. A cleaning woman working a six-hour shift should be able to cover (clean) _____ Gilbert work units.
    A. 100-200   B. 400-500   C. 1100-1200   D. 6000-7000

30. An incipient fire is one which
    A. has just started and can be readily extinguished using an ordinary hand extinguisher
    B. occurs only in motor vehicles
    C. is burning out of control in a storeroom
    D. is a banked coal fire

31. Maintaining room temperature at 75°F in the winter time will increase fuel consumption above the amount needed to maintain 70°F by APPROXIMATELY
    A. 5%   B. 10%   C. 15%   D. 20%

32. Of the following, the one which represents the BEST practical combustion condition in an oil-fired low pressure steam plant is _____ stack temperature.
    A. 8% CO_2 - 500°F
    B. 13% CO_2 - 400°F
    C. 10% CO_2 - 700°F
    D. 6% CO_2 - 400°F

33. An office has floor dimensions of 6 ft. 6 in. wide by 22 ft. 0 in. long. The floor area of this office, in square feet, is MOST NEARLY
    A. 143   B. 263   C. 363   D. 463

34. Dollies are USUALLY used
    A. as convenient platforms upon which to store items
    B. as ornamental protective covers

C. to raise items to the required level
D. to transport items from one place to another

35. When lifting a heavy object from a table, which of the following rules is it MOST important to observe?
    A. Do not bend your knees.
    B. Do not stand too close to the object.
    C. Keep your back straight.
    D. Keep your shoulder level with the object

35.____

36. The FIRST objective of all fire prevention is
    A. confining fire to a limited area
    B. safeguarding life against fire
    C. reducing insurance rates
    D. preventing property damage

36.____

37. A custodian should know the equipment used in his work well enough to
    A. make any repairs which might be needed
    B. know what parts to remove in case of breakdown
    C. anticipate any reasonable possibility of a breakdown
    D. know all the lubricants specified by the manufacturer

37.____

38. The PRIMARY responsibility of a supervising custodian is to
    A. make friends of all subordinates
    B. search for new methods of doing the work
    C. win the respect of his superior
    D. get the work done properly within a reasonable time

38.____

39. When a custodian believes that the work of a subordinate is below standard, he should
    A. assign the employee to work that is considered undesirable
    B. do nothing immediately in the hope that the employee will bring his work up to standard without any help from the supervisor
    C. reduce the privileges of the employee at once
    D. discuss it as soon as possible with the employee

39.____

40. An office worker frequently complains to the custodian that her office is poorly illuminated.
    The BEST action for the custodian to follow is to
    A. ignore the complaints as those of an habitual crank
    B. inform the worker that illumination is a fixed item built into the building originally and evidently is the result of faulty planning by the architect
    C. request a licensed electrician to install additional ceiling lights
    D. investigate for faulty illumination features in the room, such as dirty lamp globes and incorrect lamp wattages

40.____

KEY (CORRECT ANSWERS)

1.	A	11.	D	21.	A	31.	D
2.	C	12.	D	22.	C	32.	B
3.	D	13.	A	23.	C	33.	C
4.	D	14.	D	24.	B	34.	D
5.	B	15.	B	25.	D	35.	C
6.	B	16.	A	26.	D	36.	B
7.	C	17.	B	27.	A	37.	C
8.	C	18.	A	28.	C	38.	D
9.	A	19.	B	29.	C	39.	D
10.	C	20.	B	30.	A	40.	D

TEST 2

DIRECTIONS: Each question or incomplete statement is followed by several suggested answers or completions. Select the one that BEST answers the question or completes the statement. *PRINT THE LETTER OF THE CORRECT ANSWER IN THE SPACE AT THE RIGHT.*

1. Of the following, the MOST important reason for the custodian to plan work schedules for men under his supervision is that
   A. emergency situations can easily be handled if they should arise
   B. it insures that essential operations will be adequately covered
   C. the men will be more satisfied if a routine is established
   D. the relationship between the supervisor and his subordinate will be clarified

   1.____

2. Sealers for open-grained wood floors should NOT contain linseed oil because
   A. the linseed oil would damage the wood fibers
   B. the linseed oil would deteriorate mop strands
   C. water wax would penetrate the linseed oil sealer and rot the wood
   D. linseed oil on wood take too long to dry satisfactorily before a floor finish could be applied

   2.____

3. When washing painted wall areas by hand, a man should be expected to wash each hour an area, in square feet, equal to
   A. 75-125   B. 150-300   C. 400-600   D. 750-1000

   3.____

4. Of the following, the one that is MOST desirable to use in dusting furniture is a
   A. feather duster   B. paper towel
   C. counter brush   D. soft cotton cloth

   4.____

5. The one of the following floor types on which oily sweeping compound may be used is
   A. vinyl tile   B. concrete   C. linoleum   D. terrazzo

   5.____

6. A steam heating system where the steam and condensate flow in the same pipe is called a _____ system.
   A. one pipe gravity return   B. sub-atmospheric
   C. vacuum return   D. zone control

   6.____

7. A test of a boiler by applying pressure equal to or greater than the maximum working pressure is called a ____ test.
   A. hydrostatic   B. barometric   C. hygroscopic   D. gyroscopic

   7.____

8. A stack switch, as used with an oil burner,
   A. shuts down the burner in case of non-ignition
   B. shuts down the burner in case of high stack temperatures
   C. controls the flow of secondary air
   D. operates the barometric damper

   8.____

9. The vertical pipes leading from the steam mains to the radiators are called
    A. drip lines
    B. risers
    C. radiant coils
    D. expansion joints

10. Fuel oil storage tanks are equipped with vents.
    The purpose of these vents is to
    A. make tank soundings
    B. check oil flash points
    C. fill the fuel tanks
    D. allow air to mix

11. A compound gauge in a boiler room
    A. measures steam and water pressure
    B. shows the quantity of boiler treatment compound on hand
    C. measures pressures above and below atmospheric pressure
    D. indicates the degree of compounding in a steam engine

12. Of the following, the CHIEF purpose of insulating steam lines is to
    A. prevent loss of heat
    B. protect people from being burned by them
    C. prevent leaks
    D. protect the pipes against corrosion

13. The MOST important function of thermostatic traps on radiators is to
    A. regulate the heat given off by the radiators
    B. remove water and air from the radiator
    C. assist the steam pressure in filling the radiator
    D. maintain a vacuum within the radiator

14. The designation *1/8-27N.P.T.* USUALLY indicates
    A. machine screw thread
    B. pipe thread
    C. spur gear size
    D. sprocket chain size

15. The size of a chisel is determined by its
    A. length   B. width   C. pitch   D. height

16. The cause of paint blisters is USUALLY
    A. moisture under the paint coat
    B. too thick a coat of paint
    C. too much oil in paint
    D. the plaster pores not sealed properly

17. A wood-framed picture is to be attached to a plaster and hollow tile wall.
    Of the following, the PROPER installation would include the use of
    A. wire cut nails
    B. miracle glue
    C. expansion shields and screws
    D. self-tapping screws

18. The PROPER tool or method to use for driving a finish nail to the depth necessary for puttying when installing wood trim is
    A. countersink
    B. another nail of the same diameter
    C. a nail set
    D. a center punch

19. Faucet leakage in a large building is BEST controlled by periodic
    A. faucet replacement
    B. addition of a sealing compound to the water supply
    C. packing replacement
    D. faucet inspection and repair

20. Escutcheons are USUALLY located
    A. on kitchen cabinet drawers
    B. on windows
    C. around pipes, to cover pipe sleeve openings
    D. around armored electric cable going into a gem box

21. It is ADVISABLE to remove broken bulbs from light sockets with
    A. a wooden or hard rubber wedge
    B. pliers
    C. a hammer and chisel
    D. a fuse puller

22. A room 20' x 25' in area with a ceiling height of 9'6" is to be painted. One gallon of paint will cover 400 square feet.
    The MINIMUM number of gallons necessary to give the four walls and the ceiling one coat of paint is
    A. 2   B. 3   C. 4   D. 5

23. Of the following, the ones on which gaskets are MOST likely to be used are
    A. threaded pipe plugs   B. cast iron pipe nipples
    C. flanged pipe fittings   D. threaded cast iron reducing tees

24. If a 110 volt lamp were used on a 220 volt circuit, the
    A. fuse would burn out   B. lamp would burn out
    C. line would overheat   D. lamp would flicker

25. The third prong on the plug of portable electric power tools of recent manufacture is for
    A. using the tool on a 3-phase power outlet
    B. eliminating interference in radio or television sets
    C. grounding the tool as a safety precaution
    D. using the tool on direct current circuits

26. When changing brushes on a scrubbing machine, of the following, the FIRST step to take is to
    A. lock the switch in the *off* position
    B. be sure the power cable electric plug supplying the machine is disconnected from the wall outlet
    C. place the machine on top of the positioned brushes
    D. dip the brushes in water

27. In cleaning away branches that have been broken off as a result of a severe storm, one of your men comes in contact with a live electric line and falls unconscious.
    After having removed him from contact, the FIRST thing to be done is to
    A. send for an inhalator to revive him
    B. administer mouth-to-mouth resuscitation
    C. search for the switch to prevent any other such cases
    D. loosen his clothing and begin rubbing his forehead to restore circulation

28. Of the following, the MOST effective way to reduce waste in cleaning equipment and tools is by
    A. requiring a worn brush or broom to be returned before issuing a new one
    B. requiring the cleaners to use all cleaning tools for specific periods of time
    C. keeping careful records of how frequently cleaning equipment and tools are issued to cleaners
    D. making sure that cleaners use the tools properly

29. A window cleaner should carefully examine his safety belt
    A. once a week
    B. before he puts it on each time
    C. once a month
    D. once before he enters a building

30. One of your cleaners was injured as a result of slipping on an oily floor.
    This type of accident is MOST likely due to
    A. defective equipment
    B. the physical condition of the cleaner
    C. failure to use proper safety appliances
    D. poor housekeeping

31. One important use of accident reports is to provide information that may be used to reduce the possibility of similar accidents.
    The MOST valuable entry on the report for this purpose is the
    A. name of the victim
    B. injury sustained by the victim
    C. cause of the accident
    D. location of the accident

32. Fires in buildings are of such complexity that
    A. no plans or methods of attack can be formulated in advance
    B. no planned procedures can be relied on
    C. an appointed committee is necessary to direct fighting at the fire
    D. the problem must be considered in advance and methods of attack formulated

33. Of the following types of fires, a soda-acid fire extinguisher is NOT recommended for
    A. electric motor controls
    B. waste paper
    C. waste rags
    D. wood desks

34. A foam-type fire extinguisher extinguishes fires by
    A. cooling only
    B. drenching only
    C. smothering only
    D. cooling and smothering

35. If a keg of nails had on it the words *Net Weight 10 pounds*, it would mean that the
    A. keg weighed 10 pounds without the nails
    B. nails and the keg together weighed 10 pounds
    C. nails weighed 10 pounds without the keg
    D. weight of 10 pounds is approximate

36. In deciding which items should be stored together, the one of the following factors which is usually of LEAST importance is
    A. activity
    B. class
    C. cost
    D. size

37. Of the following, the MOST effective way to teach a subordinate how to store an item is to
    A. do it yourself while explaining
    B. explain the procedure verbally
    C. have him do it while you criticize
    D. let him look at photographs of the operation

38. If a cleaner is doing excellent work, then the PROPER action of the custodian is to
    A. give him preferential assignments as a reward
    B. tell the other cleaners what excellent work he is doing
    C. praise his work at the earlies opportunity
    D. do nothing since the man may become over-confident

39. A cleaner does very good work, but he has trouble getting to work on time. To get the man to come on time, you should
    A. bring him up on charges to stop the lateness once and for all
    B. have him report directly to you every time he is late
    C. talk over the problem with him to find its cause and possible solution
    D. threaten to transfer him if he cannot get to work on time

40. When the National flag is to be flown at half staff, it should ALWAYS be hoisted
    A. slowly to half staff
    B. slowly to the peak of staff and then lowered slowly to half staff
    C. briskly to the peak of staff and then lowered slowly to half staff
    D. briskly to the peak of staff and then lowered briskly to half staff

KEY (CORRECT ANSWERS)

1.	B	11.	C	21.	A	31.	C
2.	D	12.	A	22.	C	32.	D
3.	B	13.	B	23.	C	33.	A
4.	D	14.	B	24.	B	34.	D
5.	B	15.	B	25.	C	35.	C
6.	A	16.		26.	B	36.	C
7.	A	17.	C	27.	B	37.	A
8.	A	18.	C	28.	D	38.	C
9.	B	19.	C	29.	B	39.	C
10.	D	20.	D	30.	D	40.	C

EXAMINATION SECTION
TEST 1

DIRECTIONS: Each question or incomplete statement is followed by several suggested answers or completions. Select the one that BEST answers the question or completes the statement. *PRINT THE LETTER OF THE CORRECT ANSWER IN THE SPACE AT THE RIGHT.*

1. The one of the following devices that is required on BOTH coal-fired and oil-fired boilers is a(n)
   A. safety valve
   B. low water cut-off
   C. feedwater regulator
   D. electrostatic precipitator

2. Lowering the thermostat setting by 5 degrees during the heating season will result in a fuel saving of MOST NEARLY _____ percent.
   A. 2   B. 5   C. 20   D. 50

3. An electrically-driven rotary fuel oil pump must be protected from internal damage by the installation in the oil line of a
   A. discharge-side strainer
   B. check valve
   C. suction gauge
   D. pressure relief valve

4. A float-thermostatic steam trap in a condensate return line that is operating properly will allow _____ to pass and will hold back _____.
   A. steam and air; condensate
   B. air and condensate; steam
   C. steam and condensate; air
   D. steam; air and condensate

5. Changes in the combustion efficiency of a boiler can be determined by comparing changes in stack temperature and
   A. steam pressure in the header
   B. over-the-fire draft
   C. percentage of carbon dioxide
   D. equivalent direct radiation

6. The classification of the coal that is USUALLY burned in school buildings is
   A. anthracite
   B. bituminous
   C. semi-bituminous
   D. lignite

7. A boiler is equipped with the following pressurtrols:
   I. Manual-reset pressurtrol   II. Modulating pressurtrol
   III. High-limit pressurtrol
   The CORRECT sequence in which these devices should be actuated by rising steam pressure is:
   A. I, II, III   B. II, III, I   C. III, I, II   D. III, II, I

8. The temperature of the returning condensate in a low-pressure steam heating system is 195°F.
   This temperature indicates that
   A. some radiator traps are defective
   B. some boiler tubes are leaking
   C. the boiler water level is too low
   D. there is a high vacuum in the return line

9. An over-the-fire draft gauge in a natural draft furnace is USUALLY read in
   A. feet per minute
   B. pounds per square inch
   C. inches of mercury
   D. inches of water

10. The equipment which is used to provide tempered fresh air to certain areas of a school building is a(n)
    A. exhaust fan   B. window fan   C. fixed louvre   D. heating stack

11. A chemical FREQUENTLY used to melt ice on outdoor pavement is
    A. ammonia
    B. soda
    C. carbon tetrachloride
    D. calcium chloride

12. A herbicide is a chemical PRIMARILY used as a(n)
    A. disinfectant   B. fertilizer   C. insect killer   D. weed killer

13. Established plants that continue to blossom year after year without reseeding are GENERALLY known as
    A. annuals   B. parasites   C. perennials   D. symbiotics

14. A ferrous sulfate solution is sometimes used to treat shrubs or trees that have a deficiency of
    A. boron   B. copper   C. iron   D. zinc

15. A tree is described as deciduous.
    This means PRIMARILY that it
    A. bears nuts instead of fruit
    B. has been pruned recently
    C. usually grows in swampy ground
    D. loses its leaves in the fall

16. If you are told that a container holds a 20-7-7 fertilizer, it is MOST likely that twenty percent of this fertilizer is
    A. nitrogen
    B. oxygen
    C. phosphoric acid
    D. potash

17. The landscape drawings for a school indicate the planting of *Acer platanoides* at a certain location on the grounds.
    Acer platanoides is a type of
    A. privet hedge   B. rose bush   C. maple tree   D. tulip bed

18. A cleaner is attempting to lift a heavy drum of liquid cleaner from the floor to a shelf at waist height.
He is MOST likely to avoid personal injury in lifting the drum if he
    A. keeps his back as straight as possible and lifts the weight primarily with his back muscles
    B. arches his back and lifts the weight primarily with his back muscles
    C. keeps his back as straight as possible and lifts the weight primarily with his leg muscles
    D. arches his back and lifts the weight primarily with his leg muscles

19. Of the following, the BEST first aid treatment for a cleaner who has burned his hand with dry caustic lye crystals is to
    A. wash his hand with large quantities of warm water
    B. brush his hand lightly with a soft, clean brush and wrap it in a clean rag
    C. place his hand in a mild solution of ammonia and cool water
    D. wash his hand with large quantities of cold water

20. The purpose of the third prong in a three-prong electric plug used on a 120-volt electric vacuum cleaner is to prevent
    A. serious overheating of the vacuum cleaner
    B. electric shock to the operator of the vacuum cleaner
    C. generation of dangerous microwaves by the vacuum cleaner
    D. sparking in the electric outlet caused by a loose electric plug

21. Of the following, the LEAST effective method for a school custodian to use to reduce window glass breakage in his school is to
    A. keep the area near the school free of sticks and stones
    B. consult with parents and civic organizations and request their assistance in reducing breakage
    C. request that neighbors living near the school report after-hours incidents to the police department
    D. develop a reputation as a *tough guy* with the students so that they will be afraid to break windows in the school

22. The one of the following procedures that a school custodian should use when a telephone caller makes a threat to place a bomb in the school building is to
    A. hang up on the caller
    B. keep the caller talking as long as possible and make notes on what he says
    C. tell the caller he has the wrong number
    D. tell the caller his voice is being recorded and the call is being traced to its source

23. A school custodian is responsible for enforcing certain safety regulations in the school.
The MOST important reason for enforcing safety regulations is that
    A. every accident can be prevented
    B. compliance with safety regulations will make all other safety efforts unnecessary

C. safety regulations are the law, and law enforcement is an end in itself
D. safety regulations are based on reason and experience with the best methods of accident prevention

24. The safety belts that are worn by cleaners when washing outside windows should be inspected
    A. before each use
    B. weekly
    C. monthly
    D. semi-annually

25. The one of the following actions that a school custodian should take to help reduce burglary losses in the school is to
    A. leave all the lights on in the school overnight
    B. see that interior and exterior doors are securely locked at the end of the day
    C. set booby traps that will severely injure anyone breaking in
    D. set up an apartment in the school basement and stay at the school every night

KEY (CORRECT ANSWERS)

1.	A	11.	D
2.	C	12.	D
3.	D	13.	C
4.	B	14.	C
5.	C	15.	D
6.	A	16.	A
7.	B	17.	C
8.	A	18.	C
9.	D	19.	D
10.	D	20.	B

21. D
22. B
23. D
24. A
25. B

EXAMINATION SECTION
TEST 1

DIRECTIONS: Each question or incomplete statement is followed by several suggested answers or completions. Select the one that BEST answers the question or completes the statement. *PRINT THE LETTER OF THE CORRECT ANSWER IN THE SPACE AT THE RIGHT.*

1. The BEST of the following substances in which to store used paint brushes is 1.____
    A. gasoline
    B. mineral oil
    C. alcohol
    D. linseed oil

2. A CORRECT statement with respect to the use of a file is: 2.____
    A. The coarser the tooth of a file, the less metal will be removed on each stroke of the file
    B. Files are generally made to cut in one direction only
    C. When a file is used to pry apart materials, light pressure should be maintained
    D. In filing rounded surfaces, the file should rest on the work at all times

3. An ACCEPTABLE material to use on a door to overcome slight sticking to the door jamb is 3.____
    A. tallow candle   B. graphite   C. mineral oil   D. #6 oil

4. The PROPER type of wrench to use on plated or polished pipe is a(n) _____ wrench. 4.____
    A. monkey   B. pipe   C. open end   D. strap

5. Of the following, the room which requires the GREATEST amount of illumination per square foot is the 5.____
    A. library   B. gymnasium   C. auditorium   D. sewing room

6. If one of the electric bulbs in a classroom fails to light up when the switch is snapped, the trouble is MOST likely with the 6.____
    A. switch   B. wiring   C. fuse   D. bulb

7. In general, wood should be fine sanded _____ the grain. 7.____
    A. across   B. diagonal to   C. with   D. circular to

8. The reason for blowing down the water column of a boiler daily is to 8.____
    A. prevent priming or foaming in the boiler
    B. keep the passages above and below the glass clean
    C. remove lime and other mineral matter from boiler feedwater
    D. reduce the possibility of excess steam pressure from building up

9. A CORRECT step in the procedure of blowing down a low pressure boiler is:
   A. Close return valves before starting to open the blow-off valve
   B. Start the job while the boiler is in operation
   C. Add fresh water rapidly to reach the maximum level
   D. Close blow-off valve when the water reaches the lowest row of tubes

10. To determine if efficient burning of fuel is occurring, the device which is used is a(n)
    A. orsat apparatus
    B. thermostat
    C. pyrometer
    D. bourdon tube

11. The PROPER tool to use to break up clinkers sticking to the grate is a
    A. shovel   B. slice bar   C. grate bar   D. rake

12. One of the possible results of closing ash pit doors to regulate draft is
    A. warping or melting of grates
    B. reduced formation of clinkers
    C. steam will become superheated
    D. live coals will fall into the ash pit

13. Good firing methods require that
    A. the fire bed be thick enough to prevent air from passing through
    B. each side of the grate be kept bare to allow cool air to reach the stack
    C. live coals should not be allowed to burn beneath the grates
    D. the fire be stirred every hour to reduce the amount of unburned gases

14. Of the following, the one that is CORRECT with respect to the burning of hard coal is:
    A. To prevent clinkers, a hard coal fire should never be poked
    B. The fire bed should not be more than 6 inches thick at any time
    C. Air holes in the bed should be made with a rake or slice bar
    D. Infrequent heavy firing will reduce the possibility of forming holes

15. The MAIN purpose of a Hartford Loop as a return connection for a steam boiler is to
    A. remove air from the return lines
    B. prevent a boiler from losing its water
    C. allow reduction in boiler header size
    D. reduce friction in return lines

16. If a boiler fails to deliver enough heat, the MOST probable of the following reasons is the
    A. leaking of the boiler manhole
    B. boiler operating at excessive output
    C. heating surface is covered with soot
    D. unsteady water line as shown by the gauge glass

17. Generally, thermostatic traps of radiators are used to
    A. prevent the flow of water and air and allow the passage of steam
    B. prevent the passage of steam and allow the passage of water and air
    C. stop air from entering the radiator to prevent it from becoming air-bound
    D. relieve the radiator of excess steam if pressure rises too high

18. When a heating boiler is in operation, the safety valve should be tested
    A. semi-annually   B. weekly
    C. monthly   D. whenever it seems to be stuck

19. In the horizontal rotary cup oil burner, the MAIN purpose of the rotary cup is to
    A. provide air for ignition of the oil
    B. pump oil into the burner
    C. atomize the oil into small drops
    D. turn the flame in a circle to heat the furnace walls evenly

20. The BEST reason for having gaskets on manholes of a boiler is to
    A. prevent leakage from the boiler
    B. provide emergency exit for excessive steam pressure
    C. provide easy access to the boiler for cleaning
    D. prevent corrosion at manholes

21. The MAIN purpose of expansion joints in steam lines is to
    A. provide for changes in length of heated pipe
    B. allow for connection of additional radiators
    C. provide locations for valves
    D. reduce breakage of pipe due to minor movement in the building

22. If too much water is put in a boiler, the result will be
    A. excessive smoke   B. excessive rate of steam output
    C. excessive fuel consumption D. unsteady water line

23. Piping that carries condensate and air from radiators of a heating system is called
    A. dry return if above boiler water line
    B. drip line
    C. wet return if above boiler water line
    D. riser runout

24. Suppose a boiler smokes through the fire door.
    Of the following, the LEAST likely cause is
    A. dirty or clogged flues   B. inferior fuel
    C. defective chimney draft   D. air leaks into boiler

25. Of the following, the statement concerning accident prevention that is NOT correct is:
    A. Ladders should be unpainted
    B. Remove finger rings before beginning to mop
    C. Wear loose-fitting clothes when working around boilers or machinery
    D. Set ladder bottom at about 1/5 the ladder length away from the wall against which the ladder rests

KEY (CORRECT ANSWERS)

1.	D		11.	B
2.	B		12.	A
3.	A		13.	C
4.	D		14.	A
5.	D		15.	B
6.	D		16.	C
7.	C		17.	B
8.	B		18.	B
9.	B		19.	C
10.	A		20.	A

21.
22. C
23. A
24. D
25. C

TEST 2

DIRECTIONS: Each question or incomplete statement is followed by several suggested answers or completions. Select the one that BEST answers the question or completes the statement. *PRINT THE LETTER OF THE CORRECT ANSWER IN THE SPACE AT THE RIGHT.*

1. When the oil burner reset button is pressed, the burner motor does not work. The FIRST thing to check is the
    A. oil supply in oil tanks
    B. possibility of a blown fuse
    C. oil strainers which may be clogged
    D. dirty stack switch

    1.____

2. When a heating plant is laid up for the summer, one of the steps the fireman should take with respect to the boiler is to tap the brace and stay rods with a hammer.
    The MAIN reason for this is to
    A. clean these parts of accumulated rust and dirt
    B. make certain these parts are in place and not out of line
    C. remove them for storage during summer and early autumn seasons
    D. make certain they are tight and not broken

    2.____

3. In the event of a bomb threat, the custodian should take the precaution to
    A. open ash pit and fire doors of boilers
    B. pull the main switch to cut off all power in the building
    C. operate with the least number of water services possible
    D. empty water from boilers immediately after covering fire with ashes

    3.____

4. The type of fire extinguisher that requires protection against freezing is
    A. carbon dioxide   B. carbon tetrachloride (pyrene)
    C. soda acid   D. calcium chloride

    4.____

5. A CORRECT procedure in recharging soda acid fire extinguishers is:
    A. The soda charge should be completely dissolved in 28 gallons of boiling water
    B. The filled acid bottle should be tightly stoppered before it is placed back in the extinguisher
    C. The extinguisher must be recharged after use regardless of extent of use
    D. Be sure to fill container with soda solution to the top of container up to threads of cap

    5.____

6. The MOST common cause of slipperiness of a terrazzo floor after being washed is the
    A. failure to rinse floor clean after cleaning agent is used
    B. destruction of floor seal by cleaning agent
    C. incomplete removal of dirt from the floor
    D. use of oil in the cleaning process

    6.____

7. When electric lighting fixtures are washed, a precaution to observe is that
   A. the metal part of the fixture should be washed with a warm mild ammonia solution
   B. the holding screws of glass globes should be loosened about half a turn after cleaning globes
   C. trisodium phosphate should not be used in washing glass globes because it dulls glass
   D. chain links of fixture should be loosened to enable removal of entire fixture

8. Inside burns on recently cut pipe are USUALLY removed by
   A. filing   B. turning   C. reaming   D. sanding

9. When the average temperature for a day is 48°F, the number of degree days for that day is
   A. 22   B. 27   C. 12   D. 17

10. Water hammer will MOST likely occur in the
    A. self-closing valves of a drinking fountain
    B. bends in a pipe line where air can accumulate
    C. globe valve on the supply line to a fixture
    D. angle valve on the steam supply line to a radiator

11. To remove a stoppage in a trap which has not cleared by the use of a force cup, the tool to use is a(n)
    A. yarning tool   B. auger
    C. expansion bit   D. trowel

12. If the float of a flush tank leaks and fills with water, the MOST probable result will be
    A. no water in the tank   B. ball cock remains open
    C. water will flow over the tank rim D. flush ball will not seat properly

13. Fresh air inlets are GENERALLY installed in connection with a
    A. house trap   B. roof vent
    C. sump pump   D. branch soil pipe

14. The PRIMARY function of the water trap in the waste line from a wash bowl is to
    A. hold excess water from flooding waste line
    B. prevent the flow of sewer gas into the room
    C. catch particles and refuse that may enter the line with the water
    D. provide an easy means for cleaning and repairing the waste line

15. The BEST lubricant for a cylinder lock is
    A. crude oil   B. machine oil   C. tallow   D. graphite

16. A window sash holds the 16.____
    A. casing   B. glass   C. jambs   D. sills

17. The BEST procedure to follow to determine the actual cleaning ability of a 17.____
    specific material is to
    A. test its performance
    B. read the specifications
    C. ask the manufacturer
    D. examine trade literature

Questions 18-21.

DIRECTIONS: Questions 18 through 21 are to be answered on the basis of the following occurrence.

An accident occurred at P.S. 947 on Monday, January 14, resulting in the injury of a fireman-cleaner named John Jones. Jones was found unconscious on the floor of the boiler room. He showed evidence of a head injury. An ambulance was called immediately. Jones was treated by the ambulance attendant, who found no serious injury and treated the head wound. Jones, when asked about the cause of the injury, stated that he had fallen over a coal shovel lying in his path. The head injury apparently resulted from the hard contact of Jones' head with a concrete post. Jones was then taken home and was advised to check with a doctor if he felt groggy or ill. An examination of the boiler room revealed that an electric light located near the scene of the accident was out and that the area was quite dark. There were no witnesses to the accident.

18. Of the following, the information MOST necessary to make the required report 18.____
    on the accident is
    A. Jones' age
    B. Jones' work habits
    C. the name of the person who found Jones injured
    D. whether Jones was covered by Workmen's Compensation

19. When Jones was found, a safety precaution that should have been taken was 19.____
    A. extinguishing the fire in the furnace
    B. the removal of Jones to a place where the lighting was more satisfactory
    C. avoiding movement of Jones to prevent further injury
    D. raising Jones' head to restore him to consciousness

20. In accordance with Workmen's Compensation regulations, Jones has the 20.____
    right to
    A. compensation if his injuries keep him from work more than one week
    B. use any doctor provided the doctor is approved by the custodian
    C. compensation greater than the amount of his wages if he is seriously injured
    D. compensation only if he proves he did not place the shovel where it was found

4 (#2)

21. The MOST important lesson that the custodian should learn from this accident is that
    A. before an employee starts work, his place of work should be inspected by the custodian
    B. even experienced firemen-cleaners require regular weekly training in the proper performance of their duties
    C. employee should be required to turn in old burned-out electric bulb before receiving new ones
    D. regular inspections of work spaces are required to reduce accidents to a minimum

21.____

22. Information which is of the LEAST value in a report of unlawful entry into a school building is the
    A. estimated value of missing property
    B. means of entry
    C. time and date of entry
    D. general description of the school building

22.____

23. You notice several children marking an entrance door with chalk.
    The MOST desirable immediate action to take is to
    A. stop the children and tell them not to do this again
    B. ask the principal to stop the children from defacing the door
    C. take the names of the children and write to their parents
    D. remove the chalk marks, but say nothing to the children

23.____

24. Suppose that the principal advises you that there are peddlers selling their wares at sidewalk locations surrounding the school premises.
    The MOST appropriate action to take FIRST is to
    A. put up signs warning the peddlers that they are violating the law
    B. advise the peddlers that such activity on sidewalks of the school is illegal and to move on
    C. call the police immediately to clear the sidewalks
    D. suggest that the teachers tell their pupils not to patronize these unsupervised peddlers

24.____

25. A parent complains that her child refuses to use the school toilet because it is unclean.
    The FIRST step you should take upon receipt of the complaint from the school principal is to
    A. advise the principal that the toilets are kept clean and that the complaint is unwarranted
    B. tell the cleaner in charge of the floor on which the toilet is located to clean the toilet properly
    C. visit the school toilets to check on the statement made in the complaint
    D. ask the parent to see the toilets for herself rather than take the word of her child

25.____

KEY (CORRECT ANSWERS)

1.	B	11.	B
2.	D	12.	B
3.	C	13.	A
4.	C	14.	B
5.	C	15.	D
6.	A	16.	B
7.	B	17.	A
8.	C	18.	C
9.	D	19.	C
10.	A	20.	A

21.	D
22.	D
23.	A
24.	B
25.	C

EXAMINATION SECTION
TEST 1

DIRECTIONS: Each question or incomplete statement is followed by several suggested answers or completions. Select the one that BEST answers the question or completes the statement. *PRINT THE LETTER OF THE CORRECT ANSWER IN THE SPACE AT THE RIGHT.*

1. Which of the following chemicals is used to decrease the amount of oxygen in boiler water?
   A. Soda ash
   B. Sodium chloride
   C. Sodium sulfite
   D. Trisodium phosphate

2. The house tank in the basement of your school building has a pressure gauge 10 feet above the bottom of the tank.
   If a column of water weighs .434 pounds per square inch per foot and the pressure gauge reads 47 pounds per square inch, then the pressure on the booster pump at the base of the tank is MOST NEARLY, in pounds per square inch,
   A. 47   B. 52   C. 57.50   D. 51.25

3. Assume that a shipment of ammonia and bleach have just been delivered to your school and one of your cleaners asks to be instructed as to how the ammonia and bleach are to be stored.
   You should instruct him to store them
   A. *together*, because liquids are usually stored with other liquids
   B. *separately*, because shelf life is increased hen supplies are maintained in their own areas away from other supplies.
   C. *together*, because it is easier to keep an accurate inventory when supplies that are delivered together are stored together
   D. *separately*, because their containers could break and mix, creating a highly toxic gas

4. Of the following, which one is the MOST effective technique for motivating your employees?
   A. Regularly remind them that they receive a good salary and other benefits
   B. Publicly commend employees when they do good work
   C. Socialize with them during breaks and after working hours
   D. Overlook minor infractions and ignore rules that you disagree with

5. Which one of the following chemicals is used to melt ice and snow?
   A. Calcium chloride
   B. Soda ash
   C. Trisodium soot
   D. Sodium sulphite

6. Boiler *handholes* are used for
   A. climbing onto boilers
   B. lighting burners
   C. cleaning soot
   D. inspecting boilers

7. The true water level for a boiler in operation is determined by operating the
   A. pressure relief valve
   B. blow-down valve
   C. aquastat
   D. tri-cocks

8. There have been a number of illegal entries into your building during school hours, and the school principal asks you to padlock certain exit doors in the building to control such entry. You and the principal are both aware that there are laws prohibiting the padlocking of exit doors, but the principal maintains that closing off the doors in question would not impede easy exit from your building.
   You should
   A. have the doors locked as requested but also inform your supervisor as to your decision to do so and your reason for that decision
   B. refuse to have the doors locked and if the principal insists, refer him to your supervisor
   C. have the doors locked if, after looking into the matter, you determine that the remaining unlocked doors would be sufficient
   D. refuse to have the doors locked unless the principal overrules you and puts it in writing

9. You are in the boiler room when a steam line ruptures and the water in the gauge glass disappears.
   Of the following, your FIRST action should be to
   A. secure the fire
   B. shut down the vacuum pump
   C. add water to replace the escaping water
   D. secure the steam valve

10. The reading of the above gas meter diagram is
    A. 6929
    B. 6939
    C. 7929
    D. 7939

11. Sight glasses are found
    A. on air compressors
    B. in classroom doors
    C. in cross-corridor doors
    D. on vision panels

12. Graphite is USUALLY used as a
    A. lubricant
    B. cleaning compound
    C. sealant
    D. boiler water additive

13. If you receive a yearly allowance of $52,000 for your school, what would MOST NEARLY be your bi-weekly allowance if you determined that figure based on a year of 365 days?
    A. $1,925.28
    B. $1,961.30
    C. $1,994.52
    D. $2,000.00

3 (#1)

14. Number 6 fuel oil is also known as 14.____
    A. crude oil   B. bunker C oil   C. gas oil   D. kerosene

15. Of the following CO_2 readings, which one indicates the LOWEST excess in the flue gas? 15.____
    A. 10.0%   B. 12.0%   C. 14.0%   D. 15.0%

16. A large section of a ceiling in an occupied classroom is hanging loosely. Of the following, which is the FIRST action you should take? 16.____
    A. Check for leaks in the floor above
    B. Have the ceiling replastered immediately
    C. Prepare a requisition for repair
    D. Have the room evacuated

17. If you sometimes enforce rules with strong disciplinary action and at other times you enforce the same rules with mild disciplinary action, your practice is a 17.____
    A. *good* one, because it enables you to apply strict discipline to cleaners who accept it and to avoid confrontations with your more resistant workers
    B. *bad* one, because generally speaking strong disciplinary actions should be taken for infractions
    C. *good* one, because employees who are *kept guessing* about what supervisors are thinking are less likely to try to take advantage
    D. *bad* one, because discipline should be applied with consistency

18. If one of your employee's gross salary is $38,000 a year and you must deduct 5.85% of that sum, you should deduct 18.____
    A. $2,223.00   B. $2,226.00   C. $2,235.00   D. $2,342.00

19. The remote control switch of an oil-burning heating plant should be located 19.____
    A. at the boiler room exit door
    B. in the custodian's office
    C. between 2 and 5 feet from the boiler
    D. on the boiler at eye level

20. Fire Department personnel, while making a routine inspection, issue violations for conditions existing in your building. 20.____
    Of the following, it is MOST appropriate for you to
    A. explain that because schools are city property, violations cannot be issued
    B. accept the violations as written and take follow-up action
    C. inform them that they must go through proper channels before issuing the violations
    D. volunteer information about other conditions possibly in violation

21. Assume that your school building has three-phase wiring. Assume also that when you throw the start-up switch on a motor in your boiler room, the motor hums but does not turn. 21.____

4 (#1)

Of the following, the MOST likely cause for this is
A. low voltage
B. motor grounding
C. low amperage
D. a blown fuse

22. Two of your cleaners are entitled to retroactive pay of 18 cents per hour. One of the cleaners is to be paid retroactive money for 80 hours at straight time and 50 hours at time and a half. The other cleaner is entitled to 750 hours at straight time and 100 hours at time and a half.
What is the TOTAL amount of retroactive money to be paid to the two employees?
A. $238.50
B. $265.90
C. $319.50
D. $346.50

23. Of the following, the MOST likely cause of coal gas fumes is a(n)
A. improperly banked fire
B. high steam pressure
C. improper water level
D. heavy BTU content in coal being used

24. Boiler draft is measured in
A. pounds per square inch
B. degrees Fahrenheit
C. inches of water
D. cubic feet per minute

25. Of the following, which method should be used to check a CO_2 fire extinguisher?
A. Discharge it
B. Weigh it
C. Read the gauge
D. Shake it

26. A(n) _____ pump is used on a boiler system using number 6 oil
A. transfer
B. vacuum
C. ejector
D. sump

27. Your boiler water has a pH of 8. This means that the water is
A. acidic
B. neutral
C. alkaline
D. dirty

28. Assume that the high temperature on March 14 was 72°F and the low temperature was 52°F. The standard temperature for calculation of degree days is 65°F.
The number of degree days for March 4 is
A. 3
B. 7
C. 13
D. 20

29. Pig tails are commonly found on
A. steam gauges
B. water meters
C. temperature recorders
D. draft gauges

30. Your school principal complains to you that a workman making repairs to the windows in your building is making noise that is disrupting classroom instruction.

Of the following, the FIRST action you should take is to
- A. ignore the principal in the hope that the noise subsides
- B. tell the principal that there has to be a certain amount of noise when repair work is being done
- C. meet with the workman to discuss rescheduling the work in order to minimize disruption
- D. inform the workman's supervisor that you have received complaints and warn him that you will take further action if he fails to cooperate

31. *Checkerboard* floors are found in
    A. restrooms B. boiler rooms C. classrooms D. lunchrooms

32. One of your cleaners has a gross bi-weekly salary of $736.94.
    If the federal tax deduction for that period is $127.92, the state tax deduction is $42.85, and the FICA is $61.02, the city decusion is $7.36, and the state disability is $.60, what is the cleaner's net pay?
    A. $239.75   B. $362.49   C. $497.19   D. $521.03

33. The operating automatic pressuretrol shuts down the burner when the
    - A. oil pressure fluctuates due to high oil temperatures
    - B. steam pressure fluctuates due to highly acidic feedwater
    - C. oil pressure indicator arrow enters *red* or danger zone
    - D. predetermined steam pressure setting is reached

34. The PROPER method for securing lighting globes is to tighten the thumb-screws
    - A. hand tight
    - B. snug and loosen ½ turn
    - C. with pliers
    - D. till they just support the globe

35. Persons running an adult program after school hours ask to use the school kitchen to set up a large coffee maker and utensils. Board of Education policy, however, prohibits such use of the kitchen by anyone other than school kitchen workers.
    Of the following, it would be MOST appropriate for you to
    - A. explain that you are prohibited from doing so and offer an alternative
    - B. allow them to use the kitchen if you know them to be responsible and they agree to clean up afterwards
    - C. politely inform them that their request does not come under your jurisdiction
    - D. allow them to use the kitchen and afterwards have your staff clean up

36. A damaged or loose spinner cup will cause
    - A. high oil pressure
    - B. loss of lubricant
    - C. low oil pressure
    - D. poor atomization of oil

37. If, during a pay period, one of your employees works 80 hours at the straight time rate of $8.40 per hour and works 16 hours at time and a half, the employee's gross pay for the period is
    A. $739.20   B. $806.40   C. $873.60   D. $1,008.00

38. The low water cut-off stops the
   A. boiler on low water
   B. sump pump on low water
   C. sump pump in emergencies
   D. water on low pressure

   38.____

39. Which of the following chemicals is used to increase alkalinity in feedwater?
   A. Calcium chloride
   B. Sodium chloride
   C. Sodium hydroxide
   D. Hydrogen peroxide

   39.____

40. Which of the following should be used to remove mildew from marble surfaces?
   A. Bleach
   B. Ammonia
   C. Scouring powder
   D. Trisodium

   40.____

KEY (CORRECT ANSWERS)

1.	C	11.	A	21.	D	31.	B
2.	B	12.	A	22.	C	32.	C
3.	D	13.	D	23.	A	33.	D
4.	B	14.	B	24.	C	34.	B
5.	A	15.	D	25.	B	35.	A
6.	D	16.	D	26.	A	36.	D
7.	D	17.	D	27.	C	37.	C
8.	B	18.	A	28.	A	38.	A
9.	A	19.	A	29.	A	39.	C
10.	A	20.	B	30.	C	40.	A

TEST 2

DIRECTIONS: Each question or incomplete statement is followed by several suggested answers or completions. Select the one that BEST answers the question or completes the statement. *PRINT THE LETTER OF THE CORRECT ANSWER IN THE SPACE AT THE RIGHT.*

1. You have been informed that your building allowance is going to be decreased as part of a city-wide economy drive.
   Of the following, which is the FIRST action you should take in this situation?
   A. Lay-off the worker with the least seniority.
   B. Reduce the amount and complexity of your work in order to absorb the decrease.
   C. Start using less expensive supplies and materials.
   D. Study your custodial operation to determine how best to minimize the effects of the cuts.

   1.____

2. The purpose of the vent line on an oil tank is to allow
   A. water in the oil to evaporate
   B. oil to drain if tank is overfilled
   C. for expansion of the oil as the oil temperature rises
   D. gases to escape into the atmosphere

   2.____

3. A reading of 45°C is indicated on your temperature recorder.
   This temperature, expressed in degrees Fahrenheit, is
   A. 77   B. 81   C. 113   D. 145

   3.____

4. A dark orange flame in a boiler indicates
   A. low draft
   B. that the refractory is damaged
   C. too much secondary air
   D. too much primary air

   4.____

5. *Metering* faucets
   A. are washerless
   B. have aerators
   C. shut off automatically
   D. vent air

   5.____

6. You are allowed $72,000 for the operation of your building. Of this amount, your salary is $32,000, your fireman's salary is $25,000, your cleaner earns $10,500, and compensation insurance will cost $750.00.
   After these monies are paid, how much will remain?
   A. $3,150   B. $3,750   C. $4,550   D. $4,570

   6.____

7. It has come to your attention that the police department has one of your cleaners under surveillance.
   Of the following, your action should be to
   A. tell the cleaner that he is under surveillance
   B. tell all your cleaners about the situation and warn them to avoid trouble
   C. terminate the cleaner under surveillance
   D. say nothing about the situation to the cleaner

   7.____

8. After you prepared a monthly payroll report and sent it to headquarters, you find that you made errors in the report.
Of the following, it would be MOST important to
   A. do nothing since a payroll report would be thoroughly checked at headquarters
   B. make all the required changes on the copy you kept
   C. immediately resubmit the report to include the corrected information
   D. adjust the next month's figures to compensate for the error

9. Stay bolts are found in a boiler's
   A. brick setting
   B. breeching
   C. fire doors
   D. shell

10. A *plumber's friend* is used to
    A. change washers
    B. stop leaks
    C. open corroded fittings
    D. clear stoppages

11. Ballasts are found in
    A. fluorescent fixtures
    B. plumbing fixtures
    C. boiler equalizers
    D. vacuum pumps

12. You hire a person as a cleaner on the recommendation of a friend of yours who is a custodian at another school.
When dealing with the newly hired cleaner, it would be MOST appropriate for you to assign
    A. him to the same type of work as you would give to another cleaner with similar abilities
    B. less desirable work to him than you assign to other cleaners in order to avoid giving the impression that he will be receiving special treatment
    C. him work with no regard to his abilities since all workers should be treated the same
    D. him the most desirable work in order to maintain friendship with the custodian who recommended him and to encourage the newly hired cleaner to do good work

13. The size of a boiler tube is based on its
    A. inside diameter
    B. circumference
    C. outside diameter
    D. cross-sectional area

14. Of the following, the LEAST important consideration when preparing a work schedule is the
    A. number of employees on your staff
    B. type of work to be done
    C. age of the employees on your staff
    D. monies budgeted

15. A solenoid valve is also known as a _____ valve.
    A. magnetic oil
    B. thermo-electric
    C. hydraulic
    D. pressure

16. One of your employees earns $17.00 an hour and another employee earns $21.00 an hour. Last week, the employee making $17.00 an hour worked forty hours, and the employee earning $21.00 an hour worked forty-four hours. Assuming that all time in excess of forty hours a week is computed at time and a half, their combined gross pay for the week is
    A. $1,646.00   B. $1,680.00   C. $1,706.00   D. $1,752.00

17. Flame failure in a rotary up oil burner is detected by the
    A. vaporstat   B. aquastat
    C. low draft switch   D. scanner

18. If the water coming from the faucets in your building is 95°C, it is
    A. warm   B. too hot   C. tepid   D. too cold

19. You are writing a memorandum to your supervisor concerning problems you have been having with certain boiler room equipment.
    Of the following, it would be MOST important for your memorandum to
    A. be long and include proper terminology to let your supervisor know you are technically competent and knowledgeable about proper boiler plant operation
    B. explain the problem clearly and to provide possible solutions
    C. explain the problem in such a way as to avoid giving the impression that the problems are your fault or that you did not do enough to minimize the effects
    D. be respectful in tone and grammatically correct

20. One of the classrooms in your building is often littered with paper, other trash, and in otherwise unacceptable condition at the end of the day.
    Of the following, it would be MOST appropriate for you to
    A. tell the children that they are to leave the room as clean at the end of the day as they find it in the morning
    B. speak to the principal about the room's condition in order to obtain her assistance to resolve the situation
    C. advise the teacher that you will instruct your cleaners not to clean the room unless he cooperates in keeping it clean
    D. regularly check the room to determine which of the children are responsible for its condition

21. One of your employees has a gross bi-weekly salary of $600 and a FICA deduction of 5%.
    His FICA deduction for a period of 4 weeks is
    A. $3   B. $6   C. $30   D. $60

22. A(n) _____ has a gauge glass.
    A. pressure gauge   B. inspection window
    C. condensate tank   D. transom

23. One standard square of roofing shingle will cover _____ square feet.
    A. 1   B. 10   C. 100   D. 144

24. _____ are NOT a part of low pressure boilers.
    A. Crown sheets	B. Impellers
    C. Weep holes	D. Stay rods

25. If one person is normally assigned to a facility for every 33,000 square feet and you have 82,000 square feet, your manpower requirement is
    A. 1	B. 1½	C. 2	D. 2½

26. Your cleaning crew's morale is very low because the school is often vandalized, making it very difficult for your workers to maintain the building properly.
    Of the following, it would be MOST appropriate for you to tell your crew
    A. that you are aware of the effort they put in even though the building does not reflect the work they do
    B. not to work so hard because their work is not appreciated and it is a losing battle
    C. that they get paid for their work and, therefore, there is no justification for their low morale
    D. not to concern themselves about vandalism since it is a social problem, not a custodial matter

27. Nematodes are
    A. weeds	B. elevator fuses
    C. electrical circuits	D. lawn pests

28. A *supervisory* circuit is found in
    A. boiler controls	B. the principal's intercom
    C. hot water tanks	D. fire alarms

29. Braided packing is found in
    A. electrical insulation	B. stuffing boxes
    C. wall insulation	D. junction boxes

30. The gas meter in your building reads 1234 on the 1st of the month and 1356 at the end of the month.
    If the meter has a multiplier of 60, how much gas was consumed for the month?
    A. 813.60	B. 4260	C. 7320	D. 81360

31. Which of the following is NOT used to control boiler water level? A
    A. condensate return pump	B. vacuum pump
    C. blow-down valve	D. feedwater regulator

32. A water-charged fire extinguisher should NOT be used on a(n) _____ fire.
    A. paper	B. oil	C. wood	D. trash

33. A *pope's head* is used to clean
    A. floors	B. boiler tubes	C. windows	D. sidewalks

34. The drain in your school yard is stopped up after each rainfall.
Which one of the following is the MOST appropriate action to take to correct this situation.
    A. Remove the strainer basket
    B. Schedule regular drain cleaning
    C. Blank off grating
    D. Have the drain *snaked* on an annual basis

35. Of the following, which is the LARGEST size of coal?
    A. Rice   B. Buckwheat   C. Pea   D. Walnut

36. To perform a low water cut-off test, you should
    A. shut off the water at the tempering valve
    B. open the bypass valve on the feedwater regulator
    C. shut down the water supply until the boiler shuts off
    D. open the pressure relief valve

37. A recently hired cleaner does not complete tasks within the time periods that you believe to be proper for his work.
Of the following, the FIRST action you should take is to
    A. warn him that his job may be in jeopardy if he does not improve
    B. avoid mentioning anything about his work for the first few weeks of his employment
    C. ask other employees to encourage him to work harder and faster
    D. observe him while he works to determine the reasons he takes so long to complete this work

38. This year, the fuel consumption at your school has significantly increased over last year's consumption even though the weather for both years has been quite similar. You are checking your heating system to determine the reason for the increase.
Which of the following is LEAST likely to be the reason for the higher consumption?
    A. Dirty fire tubes   B. Leaking steam traps
    C. High flue gas temperature   D. High steam temperature

39. A teacher tells you that one of your cleaners broke her classroom movie projector. She states that when she left the room at the end of the preceding school day, the cleaner was working in her room and the projector was operating fine. The next morning it wasn't working.
For this situation, you should FIRST
    A. accuse the cleaner of breaking it to test his reaction
    B. order the cleaner to talk to the teacher to get the matter resolved
    C. question the cleaner to find out what, if anything, he knows about the situation
    D. watch the cleaner for several days to see if he does anything to indicate guilt

40. Of the following, which is the MOST likely indication of soot build-up in boiler tubes? 40.____
    A. A high CO_2 reading
    B. A high furnace draft reading
    C. High boiler pressure
    D. High stack temperature

KEY (CORRECT ANSWERS)

1.	D	11.	A	21.	D	31.	B
2.	D	12.	A	22.	C	32.	B
3.	C	13.	C	23.	C	33.	C
4.	A	14.	C	24.	B	34.	B
5.	C	15.	A	25.	D	35.	C
6.	B	16.	A	26.	A	36.	C
7.	D	17.	D	27.	D	37.	D
8.	C	18.	B	28.	D	38.	D
9.	D	19.	B	29.	B	39.	C
10.	D	20.	B	30.	C	40.	D

EXAMINATION SECTION
TEST 1

DIRECTIONS: Each question or incomplete statement is followed by several suggested answers or completions. Select the one that BEST answers the question or completes the statement. *PRINT THE LETTER OF THE CORRECT ANSWER IN THE SPACE AT THE RIGHT.*

1. Of the following, the BEST way for you to make sure that a cleaner understands a spoken order which you have given to him is for you to
   A. ask him to repeat the order in his own words
   B. ask him whether he has understood the order
   C. watch how he begins to follow the order
   D. ask him whether he has any questions about the order

   1.____

2. You have called a meeting with your cleaners to get their suggestions on ways to keep up cleaning standards in spite of budget cutbacks.
   You will MOST likely be successful in encouraging them to participate in the discussion if you
   A. start the meeting by giving the cleaners all your own suggestions first
   B. keep the meeting going by talking whenever the cleaners have nothing to say
   C. get the cleaners to *think out loud* by asking them for their interpretations of the problem
   D. comment on and evaluate the suggestions made by each cleaner immediately after he makes them

   2.____

3. If a custodian knows that rumor being spread by his assistants are false, he should
   A. tell the assistants that the rumors are false
   B. tell the assistants the facts which the rumors have falsified
   C. threaten to discipline any assistant who spreads the rumors
   D. find out which assistant started the rumor and have him suspended

   3.____

4. One of your cleaners tells you in private that he wants to quit his job.
   The FIRST thing you should do in handling this matter is to
   A. ask the cleaner why he wants to quit his job
   B. tell the cleaner to take a few days to think it over
   C. refer the cleaner to the personnel office
   D. try to convince the cleaner not to quit his job

   4.____

5. The MOST important reason why a custodian should seek the suggestions of his cleaners on job-related matters is that the
   A. cleaners generally have greater knowledge of job-related matters than the custodian
   B. cleaners will tend to have a greater feeling of participation in their jobs by making suggestions

   5.____

C. custodians will be able to hold the cleaners responsible for any suggestions he follows
D. custodians can win the respect of his cleaners by showing them the errors in their suggestions

6. Your supervisor has ordered you to announce to your cleaners a new cleaning rule with which you disagree.
You should
   A. admit honestly to your cleaners that you disagree with the rule
   B. announce the rule to your cleaners without expressing your disagreement
   C. encourage your cleaners by telling them you agree with the rule
   D. tell your supervisor that you refuse to announce any rule with which you disagree

7. Of the following, the BEST practice to follow in criticizing the work performance of a cleaner is to
   A. save up several criticisms and make them all at one time
   B. soften your criticism by being humorous
   C. have another cleaner, who has more seniority, give the criticism
   D. make sure that you explain to the cleaner the reasons for your criticism

8. Of the following, the BEST way to reduce unnecessary absences among your cleaners is to
   A. ask your cleaners the reason for their absence every time they are absent
   B. rely entirely on written warnings once every month to cleaners who have been absent too often during the month
   C. have your cleaners make a formal written report to you every time they are absent, explaining the reason for their absence
   D. threaten to fire your cleaners every time they are absent

9. A group of students complains to you about the lack of cleanliness in your building. You realize that budget cutbacks are unavoidably led to shortages in manpower and equipment for the cleaning staff.
Of the following, the BEST way for you to answer these students is to
   A. tell them frankly that the cleanliness of the building is none of their business as students
   B. apologize for the condition of the building and promise that your men will work harder
   C. tell them to take their complaints to the administration and not to you
   D. explain the reasons for the building's condition and what you are doing to improve it

10. The MOST important role of the school custodian in promoting public relations in the community should be to help
    A. increase understanding between the custodial staff and the community which it serves
    B. keep from community attention any failings on the part of the custodial staff

C. increase the authority of the custodial staff over the community with which it deals
D. keep the community from interfering in the operations of the custodial staff

11. A teacher conducting a class calls you to complain that the cleaners cleaning the empty classroom next to hers are being unnecessarily noisy.
    Of the following, the BEST response to the teacher is to tell her that
    A. she should go next door to tell the cleaners to stop the unnecessary noise
    B. you will tell the cleaners about her complaint and instruct them not to make unnecessary noise
    C. she should file a formal complaint against the cleaners with your superior
    D. you will come to her classroom to judge for yourself whether the cleaners are being unnecessarily noisy

11.____

12. The attitude a school custodian should generally maintain toward the faculty and students is one of
    A. avoidance   B. superiority   C. courtesy   D. servility

12.____

13. The flow of oil in an automatic rotary cup oil burner is regulated by a(n)
    A. thermostat   B. metering valve
    C. pressure relief valve   D. electric eye

13.____

14. The one of the following devices that is required on both coal-fired and oil-fired boilers is a(n)
    A. safety valve   B. low water cut-off
    C. feedwater regulator   D. electrostatic precipitator

14.____

15. The type of fuel which must be preheated before it can be burned efficiently is
    A. natural gas   B. pea coal
    C. number 2 oil   D. number 6 oil

15.____

16. A suction gauge in a fuel-oil transfer system is USUALLY located
    A. before the strainer
    B. after the strainer and before the pump
    C. after the pump and before the pressure relief valve
    D. after the pressure relief valve

16.____

17. The FIRST item that should be checked before starting the fire in a steam boiler is the
    A. thermostat   B. vacuum pump
    C. boiler water level   D. feedwater regulator

17.____

18. Operation of a boiler that has been *sealed* by the Department of Buildings is
    A. prohibited
    B. permitted when the outside temperature if below 32°F
    C. permitted between the hours of 6:00 A.M. and 8:00 A.M. and 9:00 P.M. and 11:00 P.M.
    D. permitted only for the purpose of heating domestic water

18.____

19. Lowering the thermostat setting by 5 degrees during the heating season will result in fuel savings of MOST NEARLY _____ percent.
    A. 2 B. 5 C. 20 D. 50

20. An electrically-driven rotary fuel oil pump MUST be protected from internal damage by the installation in the oil line of a
    A. discharge side strainer
    B. check valve
    C. suction gauge
    D. pressure relief valve

21. A float-thermostatic steam trap in a condensate return line that is operating properly will allow
    A. steam and air to pass and will hold back condensate
    B. air and condensate to pass and will hold back steam
    C. steam and condensate to pass and will hold back air
    D. steam to pass and will hold back air and condensate

22. Changes in the combustion efficiency of a boiler can be determined by comparing changes in stack temperature and
    A. steam pressure in the header
    B. over the fire draft
    C. percentage of carbon dioxide
    D. equivalent of direct radiation

23. The classification of the coal that is USUALLY burned in a city school building is
    A. anthracite
    B. bituminous
    C. semi-bituminous
    D. lignite

24. A boiler is equipped with the following pressuretrols:
    I. Manual-reset   II. Modulating   III. High-limit
    The CORRECT sequence in which these devices should be actuated by rising steam pressure is
    A. I, II, III B. II, III, I C. III, I, II D. III, II, I

25. The temperature of the returning condensate in a low-pressure steam heating system if 195°F.
    This temperature indicates that
    A. some radiator traps are defective
    B. some boiler tubes are leaking
    C. the boiler water level is too low
    D. there is a high vacuum in the return line

26. An over-the-fire draft gauge in a natural draft furnace is USUALLY read in
    A. feet per minute
    B. pounds per square inch
    C. inches of mercury
    D. inches of water

27. The Air Pollution Code states that no person shall cause or permit the emission of an air contaminant of a density which appears as dark or darker than number ____ on the standard smoke chart.
    A. one B. two C. three D. four

28. The equipment which is used to provide tempered fresh air to certain areas of a school building is a(n)
    A. exhaust fan
    B. window fan
    C. fixed louvre
    D. heating stack

29. When a glass globe is put back over a newly replaced lightbulb in a ceiling light fixture, the holding screws on the globe should be tightened, then loosened, one half turn.
    This is done MAINLY to prevent
    A. fires caused by electrical short circuits
    B. cracking of the globe due to heat expansion
    C. falling of the globe from the light fixture
    D. building up of harmful gases inside the globe

30. Standard 120 volt type fuses are GENERALLY rated in
    A. farads
    B. ohms
    C. watts
    D. amperes

31. A cleaner informs you that his electric vacuum cleaner is not working even though he tried the off-on switch several times and checked to see that the plug was still in the wall outlet.
    Of the following, the FIRST course of action you should take in this situation is to
    A. determine if the circuit breaker has tripped out
    B. take apart the vacuum cleaner
    C. replace the electric cord on the vacuum cleaner
    D. replace the electrical outlet

32. The one of the following that is the MOST practical method for a school custodian to use in making a temporary repair in a straight portion of a water pipe which has a small leak is to
    A. attach a clamped patch over the leak
    B. weld or braze the pipe, depending on the material
    C. drill and tap the pipe, then insert a plug
    D. fill the hole with an epoxy sealer

33. The PRIMARY function of the packing which is generally found in the stuffing box of a centrifugal pump is to
    A. compensate for misalignment of the pump shaft
    B. prevent leakage of the fluid
    C. control the discharge rate of the pump
    D. provide support for the pump shaft

34. Of the following, the MOST important reason for replacing a worn washer in a dripping faucet as soon as possible is to prevent
    A. overflow of the sink trap
    B. the mixture of hot and cold water in the sink
    C. damage to the faucet parts that can be the result of overtightening the stem
    D. air from entering the supply line

35. In carpentry work, the MOST commonly used hand saw is the _____ saw. 35._____
    A. hack B. rip C. buck D. cross-cut

36. The device which USUALLY keeps a doorknob from rotating on the spindle is a 36._____
    A. cotter pin B. tapered key
    C. set screw D. stop screw

37. The following tasks are frequently done when an office is cleaned: 37._____
    I. The floor is vacuumed.
    II. The ashtrays and wastebaskets are emptied.
    III. The desks and furniture are dusted.
    The order in which these tasks should GENERALL be done is
    A. I, II, III B. II, III, I C. III, II, I D. I, III, II

38. When wax is applied to a floor by the use of a twine mop with a handle, the 38._____
    wax should be _____ with the mop.
    A. applied in thin coats
    B. applied in heavy coats
    C. poured on the floor, then spread
    D. dripped on the floor, then spread

39. The BEST way to clean dust from an acoustical type ceiling is with a 39._____
    A. strong soap solution B. wet sponge
    C. vacuum cleaner D. stream of water

40. Of the following, the MOST important reason why a wet mop should NOT be 40._____
    wrung out by hand is that
    A. the strings of the mop will be damaged by hand-wringing
    B. sharp objects picked up by the mop may injure the hands
    C. the mop cannot be made dry enough by hand-wringing
    D. fine dirt will become embedded in the strings of the mop

KEY (CORRECT ANSWERS)

1.	A	11.	B	21.	B	31.	A
2.	C	12.	C	22.	C	32.	A
3.	B	13.	B	23.	A	33.	B
4.	A	14.	A	24.	B	34.	C
5.	B	15.	D	25.	A	35.	D
6.	B	16.	B	26.	D	36.	C
7.	D	17.	C	27.	D	37.	B
8.	A	18.	A	28.	B	38.	A
9.	D	19.	C	29.	B	39.	C
10.	A	20.	B	30.	D	40.	B

TEST 2

DIRECTIONS: Each question or incomplete statement is followed by several suggested answers or completions. Select the one that BEST answers the question or completes the statement. *PRINT THE LETTER OF THE CORRECT ANSWER IN THE SPACE AT THE RIGHT.*

1. When a painted wall is washed by hand, the wall should be washed from the _____ with a _____ sponge.   1.____
   A. top down; soaking wet
   B. bottom up; soaking wet
   C. top down; damp
   D. bottom up; damp

2. When a painted wall is brushed with a clean lambswool duster, the duster should be drawn _____ with _____ pressure.   2.____
   A. downward; light
   B. upward; light
   C. downward; firm
   D. upward; firm

3. The one of the following items which BEST describes the size of a floor brush is   3.____
   A. 72 cubic inch
   B. 32 ounce
   C. 24 inch
   D. 10 square foot

4. When a slate blackboard is washed by hand, it is BEST to use   4.____
   A. a mild soap solution and allow the blackboard to air dry
   B. warm water and allow the blackboard to air dry
   C. a mild soap solution and sponge the blackboard dry
   D. warm water and sponge the blackboard dry

5. The MAIN reason why the handle of a reversible floor brush should be shifted from one side of the brush lock to the opposite side is to   5.____
   A. change the angle at which the brush sweeps the floor
   B. give equal wear to both sides of the brush
   C. permit the brush to sweep hard-to-reach areas
   D. make it easier to sweep blackboard

6. When a long corridor is swept with a floor brush, it is good practice to   6.____
   A. push the brush with moderately long strokes and flick it after each stroke
   B. press on the brush and push it the whole length of the corridor in one sweep
   C. pull the brush inward with short, brisk strokes
   D. sweep across rather than down the length of the corrido

7. Of the following office cleaning jobs performed during the year, the one which should be done MOST frequently is   7.____
   A. cleaning the fluorescent lights
   B. dusting the Venetian blinds
   C. cleaning the bookcase glass
   D. carpet-sweeping the rug

8. The BEST polishing agent to use on wood furniture is 8.____
   A. pumice B. paste wax
   C. water emulsion wax D. neatfoot's oil

9. Lemon oil polish is used BEST to polish 9.____
   A. exterior bronze B. marble walls
   C. lacquered metal floors D. leather seats

10. Cleaning with trisodium phosphate will MOST likely damage 10.____
    A. toilet bowls B. drain pipes
    C. polished marble floors D. rubber tile floors

11. Of the following cleaning agents, the one which should NOT be used is 11.____
    A. caustic lye B. detergent
    C. scouring powder D. ammonia

12. The one of the following cleaners which GENERALLY contains an abrasive is 12.____
    A. caustic lye B. trisodium phosphate
    C. scouring powder D. ammonia

13. The instructions on a box of cleaning powder say, *Mix one pound of cleaning powder in four gallons of water.* 13.____
    According to these instructions, how many ounces of cleaning powder should be mixed in one gallon of water?
    A. 4 B. 8 C. 12 D. 16

14. In accordance with recommended practice, a dust mop, when not used, should be stored 14.____
    A. hanging, handle end down
    B. hanging, handle end up
    C. standing on the floor, handle end down
    D. standing on the floor, handle end up

15. The two types of floors found in public buildings are classified as *hard* and *soft* floors. 15.____
    An example of a hard floor is one made of
    A. linoleum B. cork C. ceramic tile D. asphalt tile

16. The BEST way for a custodian to determine whether a cleaner is doing his work well is by 16.____
    A. observing the cleaner a work for several hours
    B. asking the cleaner questions about the work
    C. asking other cleaners to rate his work
    D. inspecting the cleanliness of the spaces assigned to the cleaner

17. A chemical frequently used to melt ice on outdoor pavements is 17.____
    A. ammonia B. soda
    C. carbon tetrachloride D. calcium chloride

18. A herbicide is a chemical PRIMARILY used as a(n)
 A. disinfectant B. fertilizer
 C. insect killer D. weed killer

19. Established plants that continue to blossom year after year without reseeding are GENERALLY known as
 A. annuals B. parasites C. perennials D. symbiotics

20. A ferrous sulfate solution is sometimes used to treat shrubs or trees that have a deficiency of
 A. boton B. copper C. iron D. zinc

21. A tree described is deciduous.
 This means PRIMARILY that it
 A. bears nuts instead of fruit B. has been pruned recently
 C. usually grows in swampy ground D. loses its leaves in fall

22. If you are told that a container holds a 20-7-7 fertilizer, it is MOST likely that twenty percent of this fertilizer is
 A. nitrogen B. oxygen
 C. phosphoric acid D. potash

23. When the national flag is in such a worn condition that it is no longer a fitting emblem for display, it should be disposed of by
 A. bagging inconspicuously with other disposables
 B. burning in an inconspicuous place
 C. laundering and then using it for cleaning purposes
 D. storing for future use as a painters dropcloth

24. The landscape drawings for a school indicate the planting of *Acer platanoides* at a certain location on the grounds.
 Acer platanoides is a type of
 A. privet hedge B. rose bush
 C. maple tree D. tulip bed

25. Improper use of a carbon dioxide type portable fire extinguisher may cause injury to the operator because
 A. handling the nozzle during discharge can cause frostbite to the skin
 B. carbon dioxide is highly poisonous if breathed into the lungs
 C. use of carbon dioxide on a oil fire can cause a chemical explosion
 D. of the extremely high pressures inside the extinguisher

26. When using a portable single ladder with ten rungs, the GREATEST number of rungs that a cleaner should climb up is
 A. 7 B. 8 C. 9 D. 10

27. Of the following types of portable fire extinguishers, the one which should be used to control a fire in or around live electrical equipment is the _____ type.
    A. foam
    B. soda acid
    C. carbon dioxide
    D. gas cartridge water

28. The MOST frequent cause of accidental injuries to workers on the job is
    A. unsafe working practices of employees
    B. poor design of buildings and working areas
    C. lack of warning signs in hazardous working areas
    D. lack of adequate safety guards on equipment and machinery

29. Of the following, the MOST important purpose of preparing an accident report on an injury to a cleaner is to help
    A. collect statistics on different types of accidents
    B. calm the feelings of the injured cleaner
    C. prevent similar accidents in the future
    D. prove that the cleaner was at fault

30. A cleaner is attempting to lift a heavy drum of liquid cleaner from the floor to a shelf at waist height.
    He will MOST likely avoid personal injury in lifting the drum if he
    A. keeps his back as straight as possible and lift the weight
    B. arches his back and lifts the weight primarily with his back muscles
    C. keeps his back as straight as possible and lifts the weight primarily with his leg muscles
    D. arches his back and lifts the weight primarily with his leg muscles

31. Of the following, the BEST first aid treatment for a cleaner who has burned his hand with dry caustic lye crystals is to
    A. wash his hand with large quantities of warm water
    B. brush his hand lightly with a soft, clean brush and wrap it in a clean rag
    C. place his hand in a mild solution of ammonia and cool water
    D. wash his hand with large quantities of cold water

32. The purpose of the third prong in a three-prong electric plug used on a 120-volt electric vacuum cleaner is to prevent
    A. serious overheating of the vacuum cleaner
    B. electric shock to the operator of the vacuum cleaner
    C. generation of dangerous microwaves by the vacuum cleaner
    D. sparking in the electric outlet caused by a loose electrical wire

33. Of the following, the LEAST effective method for a school custodian to use to reduce window glass breakage in his school is to
    A. keep the area near the school free of sticks and stones
    B. consult with parents and civic organizations and request their assistance in reducing breakage

C. request that neighbors living near the school report afterhours incidents to the police department
D. develop a reputation as a *tough guy* with the students so that they will be afraid to break windows in the school

34. The one of the following procedures that a school custodian should use when a telephone caller makes a threat to place a bomb in the school is to
    A. hang up on the caller
    B. keep the caller talking as long as possible and make notes on what he says
    C. tell the caller he has the wrong number
    D. tell the caller his voice is being recorded and the call is being traced to its source

35. A school custodian is responsible for enforcing certain safety regulations in the school.
    The MOST important reason for enforcing safety regulations is because
    A. every accident can be prevented
    B. compliance with safety regulations will make all other safety efforts unnecessary
    C. safety regulations are the law and law enforcement is an end in itself
    D. safety regulations are based on reason and experience with the best methods of accident prevention

36. The safety belts that are worn by cleaners when washing outside windows should be inspected
    A. before each use
    B. weekly
    C. monthly
    D. semi-annually

37. The one of the following actions that a school custodian should take to help reduce burglary losses in the school is to
    A. leave all the lights on in the school overnight
    B. see that interior and exterior doors are securely locked
    C. set booby traps that will severely injure anyone breaking in
    D. set up an apartment in the school basement and stay at the school every night

38. The one of the following types of locks that is used on emergency exit doors is a _____ bolt.
    A. panic   B. dead   C. cinch   D. toggle

39. A telephone caller tells a school custodian that a bomb has been placed in the building and immediately hangs up the phone.
    The FIRST thing the school custodian should do, in the absence of the principal, is to
    A. call the fire department
    B. call the police department
    C. let his subordinate handle it
    D. ignore the call, since most threats are hoaxes

40. If an employee's bi-weekly salary is $1,200.00 and 6.7% is withheld for taxes, the amount to be withheld for this purpose is MOST NEARLY 40.____
    A. $62.00   B. $66.00   C. $82.00   D. $74.00

KEY (CORRECT ANSWERS)

1. D	11. A	21. D	31. D
2. A	12. C	22. A	32. B
3. C	13. A	23. B	33. D
4. B	14. B	24. C	34. B
5. B	15. C	25. A	35. D
6. A	16. D	26. B	36. A
7. D	17. D	27. C	37. B
8. B	18. D	28. A	38. A
9. A	19. C	29. C	39. B
10. C	20. C	30. C	40. C

EXAMINATION SECTION
TEST 1

DIRECTIONS: Each question or incomplete statement is followed by several suggested answers or completions. Select the one that BEST answers the question or completes the statement. *PRINT THE LETTER OF THE CORRECT ANSWER IN THE SPACE AT THE RIGHT.*

1. In city schools, wiring for motors or lighting is 1.____
   A. 208-220 volt, 4 wire, 60 cycle   B. 240-110 volt, 3 wire, 4 phase
   C. 120-208 volt, 3 phase, 4 wire   D. 160-210 volt, 4 phase, 3 wire

2. The LEAST likely cause of continuous vibration in a motor-driven pump is 2.____
   A. misalignment of motor and pump   B. loose bearings in motor
   C. poor electric connection   D. lack of graphite lubrication

3. A starter for fluorescent lights should be ordered in 3.____
   A. volts   B. amps   C. current   D. watts

4. A pipe is 50' long. If it drops ¼" each foot, how many inches does it drop in 50'? 4.____
   A. 5.5   B. 8   C. 10   D. 12.5

5. A plumber's friend operates by 5.____
   A. oscillation of water and air in the pipe
   B. density of water and pressure
   C. snake action
   D. water pressure only

6. Compound is applied to pipe thread. 6.____
   When threading pipe, where would you apply compound?
   A. Male and female thread
   B. Female only
   C. Male only
   D. At the end of the male connection only

7. A 6/32 thread refers to 7.____
   A. stove bolt   B. pipe thread
   C. machine thread   D. drill bit

8. To hang a bulletin board on plaster or hollow tile wall, use 8.____
   A. self-tapping screws   B. wire cut nails
   C. expansion shields   D. molly shank and screw

9. To relieve the vacuum on a pump, one of the following should operate: 9.____
   A. discharge valve   B. vacuum breaker
   C. foot valve   D. bleeder valve

10. When water in circulating line shows brown, the LIKELY cause is
    A. bacteria build-up
    B. rust
    C. sluggish circulation
    D. water treatment plan excessive chemical build-up

11. The purpose of rear chamber in an incinerator is for
    A. arresting sparks   B. removing noxious gases
    C. smoke reduction   D. an extra source of O_2

12. A stack switch will shut down an oil burner when
    A. the temperature of the oil is low   B. steam pressure is too high
    C. there is flame failure   D. oil pressure is low

13. A check valve in a low pressure boiler water line is to
    A. prevent contamination of boiler water
    B. prevent return flow of water
    C. equalize boiler water level
    D. prevent the pressure from increasing

14. A custodian should know
    A. how to repair equipment   B. condition before breakdown
    C. right lubrication to use D. outside conditions

15. In removing grass stains from marble and wood, which of the following should be used?
    A. Oxalic acid   B. Muriatic acid
    C. Sodium silicate   D. Disodium silicate

16. If concrete cracks appear in spring and winter, the cause is MOST likely
    A. poor concrete mix
    B. too much foot traffic
    C. poor sub-soil drainage
    D. not enough room for expansion and contraction

17. Venetian blinds should be cleaned by
    A. using feather duster   B. vacuuming
    C. washing with clear water   D. washing with cleaning solution

18. To keep chrome-plated metal clean, you should
    A. polish with fine steel wool
    B. wash with soapy water and polish with soft cloth
    C. clean with scouring powder and polish with soft cloth
    D. none of the above

19. After wetting down the floor with water solution, the BEST mop to use is
    A. a mop wet with clean water   B. one wrung out in solution water
    C. a dry mop   D. one wrung out in clear water

20. After sweeping and dusting a room, the LAST thing that should be done is 20._____
    A. empty waste basket   B. switch off lights
    C. close windows   D. clean the furniture

21. A preheater is used to heat #_____ oil. 21._____
    A. 1   B. 2   C. 4   D. 6

22. If paint blisters on the wall, the MOST likely cause is 22._____
    A. too much paint   B. porous plaster
    C. moisture in wall   D. hair-line plaster cracks

23. Cracks in newly plastered walls should be filled with 23._____
    A. putty   B. rough plaster first
    C. spackling plaster   D. silicone gel-fill

24. The BEST reason for cleaning lightbulbs is 24._____
    A. the bulb will last longer B. removing dust
    C. obtaining optimum light   D. preventing electric shock

25. The color of fire lines is 25._____
    A. yellow   B. green   C. brown   D. red

26. To neutralize acid soil, which of the following should be used? 26._____
    A. Nitrogen B. Potash   C. Phosphorus   D. Lime

27. A cleaning detergent is composed of 27._____
    A. cleaning acids   B. salts
    C. sodium compounds   D. alkaline compounds

28. The BEST method to use in watering trees and shrubs is to use 28._____
    A. jet-type velocity at roots
    B. hose with fine nozzle spray once a week and done well
    C. a hose only when needed to soak roots
    D. rotating single jet sprinkler

29. As a custodian, which of the following instructions would you give your staff 29._____
    in case of fire?
    A. Report to principal
    B. Go to location and put out fire
    C. Pull nearest fire alarm station box
    D. Make sure each one knows in advance their assigned location of duty
       when alarm rings

30. Which of the following effects does a foam extinguisher have? 30._____
    A. Smothering   B. Cooling and smothering
    C. Wetting down   D. Insulating

31. The BEST fire extinguisher to use on electric motors is
    A. soda-acid B. foam type
    C. carbon dioxide D. water

32. Two employees are arguing about their personal clothing locker. How would you handle this dispute?
    A. Reprimand both men
    B. Talk to them individually
    C. Speak to both of them together about it
    D. Write up a disciplinary report on both men

33. A fertilizer 5-10-5 means
    A. 5 potash – 10 nitrogen – phosphorous
    B. 5 tobacco chip – 10 potash – 5 phosphoric acid
    C. 5 tobacco chip – 10 nitrogen – 5 potash
    D. 5 potassium – 10 nitrogen – 5 phosphorous

34. Sand gravel mix should be
    A. 1 sand, 2 gravel, 3 cement B. 1 cement, 2 gravel, 3 sand
    C. 1 cement, 2 sand, 3 gravel D. 2 cement, 3 sand, 2 gravel

35. _____ is found between the boiler and boiler safety valve.
    A. Check valve B. No valve
    C. Steam stop valve D. Regulating valve

KEY (CORRECT ANSWERS)

1.	B	11.	C	21.	D	31.	C
2.	C	12.	C	22.	C	32.	B
3.	D	13.	A	23.	B	33.	A
4.	D	14.	B	24.	C	34.	C
5.	A	15.	A	25.	D	35.	B
6.	C	16.	D	26.	D		
7.	C	17.	A	27.	C		
8.	C	18.	B	28.	C		
9.	B	19.	C	29.	D		
10.	C	20.	B	30.	B		

TEST 2

DIRECTIONS: Each question or incomplete statement is followed by several suggested answers or completions. Select the one that BEST answers the question or completes the statement. *PRINT THE LETTER OF THE CORRECT ANSWER IN THE SPACE AT THE RIGHT.*

1. Of the following, the BEST procedure in sweeping classroom floors is:
   A. Open all windows before beginning the sweeping operation
   B. The cleaner should move forward while sweeping
   C. Alternate pull and push strokes should be used
   D. Sweep under desks on both sides of an aisle while moving down the aisle

   1.____

2. Proper care of floor brushes includes
   A. washing brushes daily after each use with warm soap solution
   B. dipping brushes in kerosene periodically to remove dirt
   C. washing with warm soap solution at least once a month
   D. avoiding contact with soap or soda solutions to prevent drying of bristles

   2.____

3. An ADVANTAGE of vacuum cleaning rather than sweeping a floor with a floor brush is that
   A. stationary furniture will not be touched by the cleaning tool
   B. the problem of dust on furniture is reduced
   C. the initial cost of the apparatus is less than the cost of an equivalent number of floor brushes
   D. daily sweeping of rooms and corridors can be eliminated

   3.____

4. Sweeping compound for use on rubber tile, asphalt tile, or sealed wood floors must NOT contain
   A. sawdust   B. water   C. oil soap   D. floor oil

   4.____

5. Of the following, the MOST desirable material to use in dusting furniture is a
   A. soft cotton cloth   B. hand towel
   C. counter brush   D. feather duster

   5.____

6. In high dusting of walls and ceiling, the CORRECT procedure is to
   A. begin with the lower walls and proceed up to the ceiling
   B. remove pictures and window shades only if they are dusty
   C. clean the windows thoroughly before dusting any other part of the room
   D. begin with the ceiling and then dust the walls

   6.____

7. When cleaning a classroom, the cleaner should
   A. dust desks before sweeping
   B. dust desks after sweeping
   C. open windows wide during the desk dusting process
   D. begin dusting at rows most distant from entrance door

   7.____

8. Too much water on asphalt tile is objectionable MAINLY because the tile
   A. will tend to become discolored or spotted
   B. may be loosened from the floor
   C. tends to disintegrate prematurely
   D. becomes too slippery to walk on

9. To reduce the slip hazard resulting from waxing linoleum, the MOST practical of the following methods is to
   A. apply the wax in one heavy coat
   B. apply the wax after varnishing the linoleum
   C. buff the wax surface thoroughly
   D. apply the wax in several thin coats

10. Assume that the water-emulsion wax needed for routine waxing in your building is 15 gallons per month. This wax is supplied in 55 gallon drums.
    To cover your needs for a year, the MINIMUM number of drums you should have to request is
    A. two   B. three   C. four   D. six

11. In washing down walls, the correct procedure is to start at the bottom of the wall and work to the top.
    The MOST important reason for this is
    A. dirt streaking will tend to be avoided or easily removed
    B. less cleansing agent will be required
    C. rinse water will not be required
    D. the time for cleaning the wall is less than if washing started at the top of the wall

12. In mopping a wood floor of a classroom, the cleaner should
    A. mop against the grain of the wood wherever possible
    B. mop as large an area as possible at one time
    C. wet the floor before mopping with a cleaning agent
    D. mop only aisles and clear areas and use a scrub brush under desks and chairs

13. A precaution to observe in mopping asphalt tile floors is:
    A. Keep all pails off such floors because they will leave water marks
    B. Do not wear rubber footwear while mopping these floors
    C. Use circular motion in rinsing and drying the floor to avoid streaking
    D. Never use a cleaning agent containing trisodium phosphate

14. The MOST commonly used cleansing agent for the removal of ink stains from a wood floor is
    A. kerosene   B. oxalic acid
    C. lye   D. bicarbonate of soda

15. The FIRST operation in routine cleaning of toilets and washrooms is to
    A. wash floors   B. clean walls
    C. clean wash basins   D. empty waste receptacles

16. To eliminate the cause of odors in toilet rooms, the tile floors should be mopped with
    A. a mild solution of soap and trisodium phosphate in water
    B. dilute lye solution followed by a hot water rinse
    C. dilute muriatic acid dissolved in hot water
    D. carbon tetrachloride dissolved in hot water

17. The principal reason why soap should NOT be used in cleaning windows is that
    A. it causes loosening of the putty
    B. it may cause rotting of the wood frame
    C. a film is left on the window, requiring additional rinsing
    D. frequent use of soap will cause the glass to become permanently clouded

18. The CHIEF value of having windows consisting of many small panes of glass is
    A. the window is much stronger
    B. accident hazards are eliminated
    C. cost of replacing broken panes is low
    D. cleaning windows consisting of small panes is easier than cleaning a window with a large undivided pane

19. Cleansing powders such as Ajax should not be used to clean and polish brass MAINLY because
    A. the brass turns a much darker color
    B. such cleansers have no effect on tarnish
    C. the surface of the brass may become scratched
    D. too much fine dust is raised in the polishing process

20. To remove chalk marks on sidewalks and cemented playground areas, the MOST acceptable cleaning method is
    A. using a brush with warm water
    B. using a brush with warm water containing some kerosene
    C. hosing down such areas with water
    D. using a brush with a solution of muriatic acid in water

21. The MOST important reason for oiling wood floors is that
    A. it keeps the dust from rising during the sweeping process
    B. the need for daily sweeping of classroom floors is eliminated
    C. oiled floors present a better appearance than waxed floors
    D. the wood surface will become waterproof and stain-proof

22. After oil has been sprayed on a wood floor, the sprayer should be cleaned before storing it.
    The usual cleaning material for this purpose is
    A. ammonia water   B. salt
    C. kerosene   D. alcohol

23. The MOST desirable agent for routine cleaning of slate blackboards is 23._____
    A. warm water containing trisodium phosphate
    B. mild soap solution in warm water
    C. kerosene in warm water
    D. warm water alone

24. Neatsfoot oil is commonly used to 24._____
    A. oil light machinery   B. prepare sweeping compound
    C. clean metal fixtures   D. treat leather-covered chairs

25. Of the following daily jobs in the schedule of a custodian, the one he should 25._____
    do FIRST in the morning is to
    A. hang out the flag   B. open all doors of the school
    C. fire boilers   D. dust the principal's office

26. When a school custodian is newly assigned to a building at the start of the 26._____
    school term, his FIRST step should be to
    A. examine the building to determine needed maintenance and repair
    B. meet the principal and discuss plans for operation and maintenance of
       the building
    C. call a meeting of the teaching and custodial staff to explain his plans for
       the building
    D. review the records of maintenance and operation left by the previous
       custodian

27. A detergent is a material used GENERALLY for 27._____
    A. coating floors to resist water
    B. snow removal
    C. insulation of steam and hot water lines
    D. cleaning purposes

28. A good disinfectant is one that will 28._____
    A. have a clean odor which will cover up disagreeable odors
    B. destroy germs and create more sanitary conditions
    C. dissolve encrusted dirt and other sources of disagreeable odors
    D. dissolve grease and other materials that may cause stoppages in toilet
       waste lines

29. To help prevent leaks at the joints of water lines, the pipe threads are 29._____
    commonly covered with
    A. tar   B. cup grease
    C. rubber cement   D. white lead

30. The advantage of using screws instead of nails is that 30._____
    A. they have greater holding power
    B. they are available in a greater variety than are nails
    C. a hammer is not required for joining wood members
    D. they are less expensive

31. Of the following, the grade of steel wool that is the FINEST is 31._____
    A. 00 B. 0 C. 1 D. 2

32. The material used with solder to make it stick better is 32._____
    A. oakum B. lye C. oil D. flux

33. In using a floor brush in a corridor, a cleaner should be instructed to 33._____
    A. use moderately long pull strokes whenever possible
    B. make certain that there is no overlap on sweeping strokes
    C. give the brush a slight jerk after each stroke to free it of loose dirt
    D. keep the sweeping surface of the brush firmly flat on the floor to obtain maximum coverage

34. A device installed in a drainage system to prevent gases from flowing into a building is called a 34._____
    A. trap B. stall C. cleanout D. bidet

35. The plumbing fixture that contains a ball cock is the 35._____
    A. trap   B. water closet
    C. sprinkler   D. dishwasher

KEY (CORRECT ANSWERS)

1. B	11. A	21. A	31. A
2. C	12. C	22. C	32. D
3. B	13. A	23. D	33. C
4. D	14. B	24. D	34. A
5. A	15. D	25. C	35. B
6. D	16. A	26. B	
7. B	17. C	27. D	
8. B	18. C	28. B	
9. D	19. C	29. D	
10. C	20. A	30. A	

EXAMINATION SECTION
TEST 1

DIRECTIONS: Each question or incomplete statement is followed by several suggested answers or completions. Select the one that BEST answers the question or completes the statement. *PRINT THE LETTER OF THE CORRECT ANSWER IN THE SPACE AT THE RIGHT.*

1. Two cleaners swept four corridors in 24 minutes. Each corridor measured 12 feet x 176 feet.
   The space swept per man per minute was MOST NEARLY _____ square feet.

   A. 50   B. 90   C. 180   D. 350

2. The BEST time of the day to dust classroom furniture and woodwork is

   A. in the morning before the students arrive
   B. during the morning recess
   C. during the students' lunch time
   D. immediately after the students are dismissed for the day

3. A custodian-engineer wishes to order sponges in the most economical manner. Keeping in mind that large sponges can be cut up into many smaller sizes, the one of the following that has the LEAST cost per cubic inch of sponge is

   A. 2" x 4" x 6" sponges @ $0.24
   B. 4" x 8" x 12" sponges @ $1.44
   C. 4" x 6" x 36" sponges @ $4.80
   D. 6" x 8" x 32" sponges @ $9.60

4. Many new products are used in new schools for floors, walls, and other surfaces. A custodian-engineer should determine the BEST procedure to be used to clean such new surfaces by

   A. referring to the board of education's manual of procedures
   B. obtaining information on the cleaning procedure from the manufacturer
   C. asking the advice of the mechanics who installed the new material
   D. asking the district supervisor how to clean the surfaces

5. The one of the following chemicals that a custodian-engineer should tell a cleaner to use to remove mildew from terrazzo is

   A. ammonia   B. oxalic acid
   C. sodium hypochlorite D. sodium silicate

6. The type of soft floor that is basically a mixture of oxidized linseed oil, resin, and ground cork pressed upon a burlap backing is known as

   A. asphalt tile   B. cork tile
   C. linoleum   D. vinyl tile

7. The difficulty of cleaning soil from surfaces is LEAST affected by the

   A. length of time between cleanings
   B. chemical nature of the soil

63

C. smoothness of the surface being cleaned
D. standard time allotted to the job

8. The one of the following cleaning agents that is GENERALLY classified as an alkaline cleaner is

   A. sodium carbonate
   B. ground silica
   C. kerosene
   D. lemon oil

9. The one of the following cleaning agents that should be used ONLY when adequate ventilation and protective measures have been taken is

   A. methylene chloride
   B. sodium chloride
   C. sodium carbonate
   D. calcium carbonate

10. Of the following, the MOST important consideration in the selection of a cleaning agent is the

    A. cost per pound or gallon
    B. amount of labor involved in its use
    C. wording of the manufacturer's warranty
    D. length of time the manufacturer has been producing cleaning agents

11. The fan motor in a central vacuum cleaner system is found to be operating at 110% of its rated capacity.
    The one of the following actions which is MOST likely to decrease the load on the motor is

    A. tying-back several outlets in the open position on each floor
    B. moving the butterfly damper slightly toward the closed position
    C. removing ten percent of the filter bags
    D. operating the bag shaker continuously

12. A groundskeeper asks how to remove an accumulation of grease from the concrete near the loading dock.
    Of the following, the cleaning agent that a custodian-engineer should tell him to use to degrease the area is a(n)

    A. acid cleaner
    B. alkaline cleaner
    C. liquid soap
    D. solvent cleaner

13. The instructions for mixing a powdered cleaner in water state, *Mix three ounces of powder in a 14-quart pail three-quarters full of water.*
    A cleaner asks you how much powdered cleaner he should use in a mop truck containing 28 gallons of water to obtain the same strength solution. Your answer should be _____ ounces of powder.

    A. 6
    B. 8
    C. 24
    D. 32

14. A resin-base floor finish USUALLY

    A. gives the highest lustre of all floor finishes
    B. should be applied in one heavy coat
    C. provides a slip-resistant surface
    D. should not be used on asphalt tile

15. The one of the following cleaning operations on soft floors that generally requires MOST NEARLY the same amount of time per 1,000 square feet as damp mopping is

    A. applying a thin coat of wax
    B. sweeping
    C. dust mopping
    D. wet mopping

16. Of the following cleaning jobs, the one that should be allowed the MOST time to complete a 1,000 square foot area is

    A. vacuuming carpets
    B. washing painted walls
    C. stripping and waxing soft floors
    D. machine-scrubbing hard floors

17. When instructing your staff in the use of sodium silicate, you should tell them that it is MOST commonly used to

    A. seal concrete floors
    B. condition leather
    C. treat boiler water
    D. neutralize acid wastes

18. Cleaners should be instructed that dust mopping is LEAST appropriate for removing light soil from _____ floors.

    A. terrazzo
    B. unsealed concrete
    C. resin-finished soft
    D. sealed wood

19. Of the following, the substance that should be recommended for polishing hardwood furniture is

    A. lemon oil polish
    B. neat's-foot oil
    C. paste wax
    D. water-emulsion wax

20. The use of concentrated acid to remove stains from ceramic tile bathroom floors USUALLY results in making the surface

    A. pitted and porous
    B. clean and shiny
    C. harder and glossier
    D. waterproof

21. Asphalt tile floors should be protected by coating them with

    A. hard-milled soap
    B. water-emulsion wax
    C. sodium metaphosphate
    D. varnish

22. Of the following, the BEST way to economize on cleaning tools and materials is to

    A. train the cleaners to use them properly
    B. order at least a three-year supply of every item in order to avpid annual price increases
    C. attach a price sticker to every item so that the people using them will realize their high cost
    D. delay ordering material for three months at the beginning of each year to be sure that the old material is used to the fullest extent

23. The MINIMUM amount of free chlorine that swimming pool water should contain for proper disinfection is _____ parts per million.

    A. 1.0   B. 10   C. 50   D. 500

24. The point at which swimming pool filters should be back-washed is when the difference between the inlet and outlet pressures EXCEEDS _____ psi.

    A. 5   B. 10   C. 15   D. 20

25. An orthotolidine test is used to test a water sample to see what quantity it contains of

    A. alum   B. ammonia   C. chlorine   D. soda ash

26. The ideal flue gas temperature in a rotary-cup oil-fired boiler should be equal to the steam temperature PLUS

    A. 50° F   B. 125° F   C. 275° F   D. 550° F

27. The carbon dioxide reading in a boiler flue when the boiler is operating efficiently should be MOST NEARLY

    A. 0.5 inches of water   B. 8 ounces per mol
    C. 10 psi   D. 12 percent

28. The one of the following that PRIMARILY indicates a low water level in a steam boiler is the

    A. pressure gauge   B. gauge glass
    C. safety valve   D. hydrometer

29. The one of the following steps that should be taken FIRST if a safety valve on a coal-fired steam boiler pops off is to

    A. add water to the boiler
    B. reduce the draft
    C. tap the side of the safety valve with a mallet
    D. open the bottom blow-off valve

30. A device that operates to vary the resistance of an electrical circuit is USUALLY part of a _____ pressurtrol.

    A. high-limit   B. low-limit
    C. manual-reset   D. modulating

KEY (CORRECT ANSWERS)

1.	C	16.	C
2.	A	17.	A
3.	B	18.	B
4.	B	19.	C
5.	C	20.	A
6.	C	21.	B
7.	D	22.	A
8.	A	23.	A
9.	A	24.	B
10.	B	25.	C
11.	B	26.	B
12.	D	27.	D
13.	D	28.	B
14.	C	29.	B
15.	A	30.	D

TEST 2

DIRECTIONS: Each question or incomplete statement is followed by several suggested answers or completions. Select the one that BEST answers the question or completes the statement. *PRINT THE LETTER OF THE CORRECT ANSWER IN THE SPACE AT THE RIGHT.*

1. A solenoid valve is actuated by

    A. air pressure
    B. electric current
    C. temperature change
    D. light rays

2. A sequential draft control on a rotary-cup oil-fired boiler should operate to

    A. *open* the automatic damper at the end of the post-purge perio'd
    B. *open* the automatic damper when the draft has increased during normal burner operation
    C. *close* the automatic damper just before the burner motor starts up
    D. *close* the automatic damper after the burner goes off and the burner cycle is completed

3. The one of the following components of flue gas that indicates, when present, that more excess air is being supplied than is being used is

    A. carbon dioxide
    B. carbon monoxide
    C. nitrogen
    D. oxygen

4. An advantage that a float-thermostatic steam trap has over a float-type steam trap of comparable rating is that a float-thermostatic trap

    A. requires less maintenance
    B. is easier to install
    C. allows non-condensable gases to escape
    D. releases the condensate at a higher temperature

5. A pump delivers 165 pounds of water per minute against a total head of 100 feet. The water horsepower of this pump is _____ HP.

    A. 1/2   B. 2   C. 5   D. 20

6. Of the following, the BEST instrument to use to measure over-the-fire draft is the

    A. Bourdon tube gauge
    B. inclined manometer
    C. mercury manometer
    D. potentiometer

7. The temperature of the water in a steam-heated domestic hot water tank is controlled by a(n)

    A. aquastat
    B. thermostatic regulating valve
    C. vacuum breaker
    D. thermostatic trap

8. The one of the following conditions that will MOST likely cause fuel oil pressure to fluctuate is

    A. a faulty pressure gauge
    B. a clean oil-strainer
    C. cold oil in the suction line
    D. an over-tight pump drive belt

9. The cooler in a Freon 12 refrigeration system that is equipped with automatic protective devices is MOST likely to be accidentally damaged by water freeze-up when the system('s)

    A. is operating at reduced load
    B. is operating at rated load
    C. condenser water-flow is interrupted
    D. is being pumped down

10. The capacity of a water-cooled condenser is LEAST affected by the

    A. water temperature
    B. refrigerant temperature
    C. surrounding air temperature
    D. quantity of condenser water being circulated

11. Of the following chemicals used in boiler feedwater treatment, the one that should be used to RETARD corrosion in the boiler circuit due to dissolved oxygen is sodium

    A. aluminate   B. carbonate   C. phosphate   D. sulfite

12. The heating system in a certain school is equipped with vacuum return condensate pumps.
    The MOST likely place for an air-vent valve to be installed in this plant is on

    A. each radiator
    B. the outlet of the domestic hot water steam heating coil
    C. the pressure side of the vacuum pump
    D. the shell of the domestic hot water tank

13. *Priming* of a steam boiler is NOT caused by

    A. load swings
    B. uneven fire distribution
    C. too high a water level
    D. high alkalinity of the boiler water

14. A Hartford loop is used in school heating systems PRIMARILY to

    A. provide for thermal expansion of the steam distribution piping
    B. equalize the water level in two or more boilers
    C. prevent siphoning of water out of the boiler
    D. by-pass the electric fuel-oil heaters when the steam heaters are operating

15. Of the following, the MOST likely use for temperature-indicating crayons by a custodian-engineer is in

    A. checking the operation of the radiator traps
    B. replacing room thermometers that have been vandalized
    C. indicating possible sources of spontaneous combustion
    D. checking the effectiveness of an insulating panel

16. A stop-and-waste cock is GENERALLY used on

    A. refrigerant lines between the compressor and the condenser
    B. soil lines
    C. gas supply lines
    D. water lines subjected to low temperatures

17. A pressure-regulating valve in a compressed air line should be preceded by a(n)

    A. check valve   B. intercooler
    C. needle valve   D. water-and-oil separator

18. A house trap is a fitting placed in the house drain immediately inside the foundation wall of a building.
    The MAIN purpose of a house trap is to

    A. prevent the entrance of sewer gas into the building drainage system
    B. provide access to the drain lines in the basement for cleaning
    C. drain the basement in case of flooding
    D. maintain balanced air pressure in the fixture traps

19. The one of the following that is BEST to use to smooth a commutator is

    A. Number 1/0 emery cloth   B. Number 00 sandpaper
    C. Number 2 steel wool   D. a safe edge file

20. The electric service that is provided to MOST schools in the city is NOMINALLY

    A. 208 volt-3 phase -4 wire - 120 volts to ground
    B. 208 volt-3 phase -3 wire - 208 volts to ground
    C. 220 volt-2 phase -3 wire - 110 volts to ground
    D. 440 volt-3 phase -4 wire - 240 volts to ground

21. All the fuses in an electrical panel are good but the clips on the fuse in circuit No. 1 are much hotter than the clips of the other fuses.
    Of the following, the MOST likely cause of this condition is that

    A. circuit No. 1 is greatly overloaded
    B. circuit No. 1 is carrying much less than rated load
    C. the room temperature is abnormally high
    D. the fuse in circuit No. 1 is very loose in its clips

22. Of the following, the BEST tool to use to drive a lag screw is a(n)

    A. open-end wrench   B. Stillson wrench
    C. screwdriver   D. alien wrench

23. Of the following, the one that is MOST likely to be used in landscaping work as ground cover is

    A. Barberry   B. Forsythia
    C. Pachysandra   D. Viburnum

24. The velocity of air in a ventilation duct is USUALLY measured with a(n)

    A. hydrometer   B. psychrometer
    C. pyrometer   D. pitot tube

4 (#2)

25. The motor driving a centrifugal pump through a direct-connected flexible coupling burned out.
    When a new motor is ordered, it is important to specify the same NEMA frame size so that the

    A. horsepower will be the same
    B. speed will be the same
    C. conduit box will be in the same location
    D. mounting dimensions will be the same

25.____

26. A custodian-engineer should inspect the school building for safety

    A. at least once each day
    B. at least every other day
    C. at least once a week
    D. at the end of each vacation period

26.____

27. Of the following, the MOST important practice to follow in order to prevent fires in a school is to train the staff to

    A. fight fires of every kind
    B. detect and eliminate every possible fire hazard
    C. keep halls, corridors, and exits clear
    D. place flammables in fire-proof containers

27.____

28. The one of the following types of portable fire extinguishers that is MOST effective in fighting an oil fire is the _____ type.

    A. soda-acid   B. loaded-stream
    C. foam   D. carbon dioxide

28.____

29. A custodian-engineer opens the door to the boiler room and discovers that fuel oil has leaked onto the floor and caught fire.
    Of the following, the FIRST action he should take is to

    A. notify the Principal
    B. notify the fire department
    C. turn off the remote control switch
    D. fight the fire using a Class B extinguisher

29.____

30. The MINIMUM noise level beyond which hearing may be impaired is _____ decibels.

    A. 10   B. 50   C. 90   D. 130

30.____

KEY (CORRECT ANSWERS)

1.	B		16.	D
2.	D		17.	D
3.	D		18.	A
4.	C		19.	B
5.	A		20.	A
6.	B		21.	D
7.	B		22.	A
8.	C		23.	C
9.	D		24.	D
10.	C		25.	D
11.	D		26.	A
12.	B		27.	B
13.	D		28.	C
14.	C		29.	C
15.	A		30.	C

EXAMINATION SECTION
TEST 1

DIRECTIONS: Each question or incomplete statement is followed by several suggested answers or completions. Select the one that BEST answers the question or completes the statement. *PRINT THE LETTER OF THE CORRECT ANSWER IN THE SPACE AT THE RIGHT.*

1. The BEST course of action to take to settle a job-related dispute that has arisen among two of your employees is to

    A. bring them both together, listen to their arguments, and then make a decision
    B. tell the two employees individually to settle their dispute
    C. tell both employees to submit their dispute in writing to you and then make a decision
    D. listen to the argument of each one separately and then make a decision

    1._____

2. A custodian accidentally discovers a bottle of whiskey in a staff member's desk. The BEST procedure for the custodian to follow is to

    A. verbally reprimand him and prefer departmental charges
    B. inform him that whiskey is not allowed in school buildings
    C. call a meeting of all the employees and tell them what you found
    D. do nothing as you do not want to embarrass the person

    2._____

3. A new employee under your supervision constantly reports late for work. The one of the following actions you should take FIRST is to

    A. admonish him in front of the other employees
    B. prefer charges against him
    C. transfer him to another school
    D. warn him that he must be on time

    3._____

4. The one of the following procedures that is BEST to follow when it is necessary to reprimand a worker is to

    A. issue the same reprimand to all your men
    B. avoid him so he won't feel bad
    C. speak to him privately about the matter
    D. tell him what he has done wrong immediately to teach the other employees a lesson

    4._____

5. The LEAST important factor to consider when evaluating the work of an employee is

    A. his grade on his civil service test
    B. the quality of his work
    C. his resourcefulness
    D. his attendance record

    5._____

6. The one of the following supervisory actions that a custodian should use LEAST often is to

   A. make periodic reports to his superior about the work of his men
   B. bring employees up on "charges" whenever they do anything wrong
   C. listen to staff grievances
   D. advise an employee concerning a personal problem

7. The MAIN supervisory responsibility of a custodian is to

   A. foster policies of the board and the parents' organizations
   B. do his job so well that the students and employees like him
   C. make assignments to his employees
   D. keep the building and grounds in good operating condition

8. One of your employees verbally protests to you about your evaluation of his work. The BEST way to handle him is to

   A. advise him of your lengthy and qualified experience
   B. tell him that you do not care to talk about it
   C. explain to him how you arrived at your evaluation
   D. tell him that since all the other employees are satisfied, he should withdraw his complaint

9. A custodian will BEST keep the morale of his men high by

   A. giving praise for well-done work
   B. assigning good workers the most work
   C. personally helping each man in all the details of the man's job
   D. allowing special privileges for good work

10. In training maintenance personnel under the supervision of a custodian, the one of the following that should be given LEAST consideration by the custodian is

    A. how the training is to be given
    B. who is to be trained
    C. when the training will be given
    D. how the school principal wants them to be trained

11. The BEST attitude for a custodian to follow in his dealings with the public is to

    A. offer aid and cooperation to the public wherever possible
    B. show authority so that the public knows the limits to which they may make requests
    C. ignore the public since the custodian has a specific job to do
    D. refer the public to higher authority for solution of all their problems

12. The students playing in the schoolyard consistently lose rubber balls that land on the school roof. They request that you, the custodian, retrieve these balls
Of the following, the BEST procedure for you to follow is .

    A. teach them a lesson and refuse to retrieve the balls
    B. retrieve the balls and throw them into the incinerator
    C. one day a week retrieve the balls and return them to the students
    D. retrieve the balls and give them to a local children's charity

13. The president of a charitable organization requests a permit to use the school building. You, the custodian, note that this same organization used the school previously and did not observe the "no smoking" rules.
    The BEST procedure for you to follow is to

    A. deny the organization a permit since they did not obey the school regulations before
    B. issue the permit without any questions since a large group is difficult to control
    C. inform the president that if any of his members continue to disregard the "no smoking" rules, future permits will not be issued
    D. inform the president that if any of his members continue to disregard the "no smoking" rules, you will evict them from the school building

14. Due to some grievances, parents occupy your school on a weekend and refuse to leave. As the school principal is out of town and unavailable, the BEST procedure for you, the custodian on duty, is to

    A. tell your employees to vacate the school
    B. call the police department
    C. cooperate with the parents on the take-over
    D. lock all the people in the school

15. An organization requests a permit to use the school auditorium from the hours of 7 P.M. to 10 P.M. on a Tuesday evening. The organization also requests that its members be allowed to enter the school earlier than 7 P.M. and leave later than 10 P.M.
    The BEST procedure for you, the custodian, to follow is to

    A. inform the organization leader that the organization may only use the school from the hours of 7 P.M. to 10 P.M.
    B. issue the permit without saying anything as you want to maintain good public relations
    C. refer the matter to the school principal as you do not want to get involved
    D. ask the organization leader the reasons for the request and, if the request is fair, issue the permit and let the organization do as it pleases

16. Dog owners in the neighborhood have been disregarding the *curb your dog* signs and walking their dogs on your school lawn. You find that this interferes with the operation of powered lawn mowing equipment.
    Your BEST procedure to follow is to

    A. put up a higher fence
    B. chase the people and dogs away
    C. tell the owners you will call the police department
    D. explain the problem to the owners and ask them to curb their dogs

17. A cleaner reports to the custodian that a particular schoolroom is consistently messy and dirty. The one who is equally at fault as the students for this dirty room is the

    A. students' parents
    B. regular classroom teacher
    C. student peer groups
    D. cleaner for reporting the matter

18. A parent walks into a custodian's office and starts to shout at him about a claimed injustice to her child. The PROPER procedure for the custodian to follow is to

    A. call the police department
    B. summon the security guards
    C. vacate the office
    D. escort the parent to a guidance counselor

19. A newspaper reporter visiting a school should normally be referred to the

    A. school principal
    B. school custodian engineer
    C. assistant superintendent of schools
    D. borough supervisor of school custodians

20. The parents of children in the neighborhood of your school complain to you that their children cannot use the school playground after school hours because the gates are closed. The BEST procedure for you to follow is

    A. tell the parents the gates will remain closed after school hours
    B. arrange for the children to use a play street
    C. tell the parents to meet with the board on this matter
    D. try to arrange for the school gates to be open to a later hour after school hours

21. Assume that there is a regulation requiring the men to notify the custodian when they intend to be absent. One of your men stays out without notifying you.
    Of the following, the FIRST thing that you should do is to

    A. discuss the matter with your supervisor
    B. find out the reason for the man's failure to comply with this regulation
    C. threaten the man with disciplinary action
    D. find out what the other custodians are doing about similar situations

22. The members of a crew are LEAST likely to object to strict rules as long as

    A. they know who made them
    B. the rules are applied only occasionally as a disciplinary measure
    C. the rules are applied equally to all the workers
    D. they are posted in a public place

23. Your supervisor complains to you that he could not find you at your assigned location and that the crew under your supervision was idle while you were away.
    Of the following, it is MOST important for you to

    A. improve your supervisory practices
    B. warn the men to look busy whenever they see one of the bosses
    C. disregard such an unreasonable complaint
    D. make certain you are rarely away from your assigned location

24. Assume that the crew you supervise considers some of their routine work unpleasant. The BEST way to get these unpleasant tasks done is to

    A. rotate them among all your men
    B. assign them to easygoing workers who never complain
    C. use them as a means of disciplining habitual latecomers
    D. do them yourself

25. Assume that when a custodian arrives at a job location, he finds that a loud argument is going on between two of his men.
    Of the following, the MOST advisable action for him to take first is to

    A. send one of the men to another job
    B. find out what caused the argument
    C. ask one of the other men to tell him the cause of the argument
    D. take the men with him to his supervisor

KEY (CORRECT ANSWERS)

1.	A	11.	A
2.	B	12.	C
3.	D	13.	C
4.	C	14.	B
5.	A	15.	A
6.	B	16.	D
7.	D	17.	B
8.	C	18.	D
9.	A	19.	A
10.	D	20.	D

21. B
22. C
23. A
24. A
25. B

TEST 2

DIRECTIONS: Each question or incomplete statement is followed by several suggested answers or completions. Select the one that BEST answers the question or completes the statement. *PRINT THE LETTER OF THE CORRECT ANSWER IN THE SPACE AT THE RIGHT.*

1. Of the following, the BEST reason for a custodian NOT allowing his employees to accept tips from people is that

    A. all employees would not be given equal treatment
    B. employees would become dishonest
    C. people are entitled to service without tips
    D. people in projects can't afford tips

    1.____

2. Your attitude as a custodian to complaints by your employees should be that

    A. all employees like to complain
    B. if you let the worker "give off some steam," the complaint will disappear
    C. you will listen to them and try to correct the condition
    D. you will try to show the worker where he is wrong

    2.____

3. A requisition would be filled out by a custodian in order to

    A. get supplies from the stockroom
    B. return to the stockroom supplies you haven't used
    C. find out the supplies you have on hand
    D. show that supplies were used up faster than expected

    3.____

4. Assume that you are a custodian and have to write a report on a new employee who will finish his probationary period next month.
   Which one of the following would be the BEST reason for recommending that he be dropped from the job? He

    A. was late several times during the past five months for a total of 50 minutes
    B. is a slow worker compared to the other men
    C. insists on eating his lunch alone instead of with the other men
    D. is in the habit of accepting drinks from outsiders during working hours although you have often told him it is forbidden

    4.____

5. It is MOST important that a report from a custodian to his superior be

    A. typewritten
    B. free of any mistakes in spelling or English
    C. accurate and have all the necessary facts
    D. brief to save time of all concerned

    5.____

6. Suppose that you are a custodian and one of your men asks why you did not recommend him for an above-average work performance rating.
   You should tell him

    A. that above-average work reports can be recommended only by higher authority
    B. why you did not give him an above-average work report
    C. that you will recommend an above-average v/ork performance rating next year if he does better work
    D. how he can appeal his rating and help him write his appeal

    6.____

7. Suppose that you are a custodian and one of your men is absent from work one day. You don't have any extra men and some of the work usually done by the absent man has to be finished that day.
It would be BEST for you to

   A. call your men together and let them decide which one is to do the work
   B. shorten the lunch period and have each man do some of the work
   C. ask one of your better men to *pitch in* by doing a little extra work today
   D. explain to the buildings superintendent why it will not be possible to finish this work today

8. One of your men complains about a job you gave him. He is angry about getting the assignment. You don't think that the man is right in getting so upset.
You should

   A. discuss the problem with him and explain why you gave him the job
   B. refer the man to your supervisor because he refuses to obey orders
   C. show the man that the whole matter is unimportant and a waste of time
   D. tell the man to do the job first and complain later

9. Two of your men start an argument while at work. As a custodian, you should

   A. ignore them; it is normal for men working together to have arguments
   B. stop them right away and find out what started the argument
   C. let them argue it out as long as they continue working and don't talk too loud
   D. speak to one of the men privately and tell him he is interfering with the work

10. Suppose you are a new custodian and you are put in charge of a crew of men whom you do not know and who have been working together for a few months.
For a smooth changeover to your leadership, it would be BEST for you to

    A. let them continue working at their present assignments while you get to know them better
    B. tell the men to call their old supervisor if they have any trouble while you are learning the job
    C. ask the most experienced man to take charge of the crew for a short while until you are more familiar with the work
    D. ask each man whether he is satisfied with what he is doing or wants a change

11. One of your men makes a suggestion for improving the method of doing the work. You don't think the suggestion is workable.
You should, as a custodian,

    A. forget the idea since it isn't workable
    B. tell the man to try out the idea and hold him responsible if it doesn't work out
    C. discuss with the man why you think the idea won't work and praise him for his interest in the job
    D. point out to the man that he is wasting your time bringing up an idea that is not practical

12. Suppose that you and your supervisor are making an inspection of one of the buildings you are responsible for cleaning. Your superior notices that the elevator in the building has not been cleaned. You know that a new employee who has been on the job for only three months is assigned to this building. You should

    A. tell your supervisor that you will have the elevator cleaned and see that it is kept clean in the future
    B. explain to your supervisor the trouble you have in training new employees
    C. find the new man and ask him to explain to you and your superior why the elevator is not clean
    D. tell your supervisor that the elevator was clean when you made your last inspection

13. Suppose that your men were asked to work overtime in order to repair a water main break. When the work is finished, your superior thanks you for the excellent work that was done.
    For you, a custodian, to tell your men about this would be

    A. *bad,* because this was a private conversation between you and your superior
    B. *good,* because your men will see that you are well-liked by your superior
    C. *bad,* because your men will think that they will be asked to work whenever there is an emergency
    D. *good,* because it will show the men their cooperation is appreciated

14. When you, as a custodian, discuss a grievance with an employee, you should

    A. not tell the employee what you think of his complaint until a later date
    B. avoid any arguments with the employee
    C. convince the employee that there is no basis for this grievance
    D. tell the employee his complaint is justified

15. At a quarter to five, one of your employees tells you that the incinerator in his building has much refuse in it and he is willing to work overtime to burn it.
    If you give him permission to do this, it would be

    A. *good,* because it will save time the next day for other important work
    B. *bad,* because this is not an emergency for which overtime could be approved
    C. *good,* because tenants would not complain that refuse piles up and causes odors
    D. *bad,* because the law does not allow burning after 5:00 P.M.

16. Because of absences, you are left short-handed.
    Which one of the following operations should you lay over so that you can cover the MOST important work on a minimum basis?

    A. Incineration of garbage
    B. Sweeping the lobby
    C. Sweeping and washing the elevators
    D. Washing corridor windows

17. Suppose that one of your men who is doing good work asks for a transfer to another custodian.
It would be BEST for you to

    A. have a private talk with the man to find out why he wants a transfer
    B. tell the man that the other custodian will also expect him to do good work
    C. approve the transfer without question because a dissatisfied man will do a poor job
    D. ask the other men in your crew if they are dissatisfied with your supervision

17.____

18. One of your experienced workers and a new employee are arguing about the correct way to do a job on which they are working together.
As a custodian, you should

    A. listen to both men and then tell them that they must learn to settle their argument without interrupting your work
    B. side with the older worker because he is more experienced
    C. listen to both men and then tell them how the work is to be done
    D. take one of the men off the job

18.____

19. Suppose that the department is introducing a new procedure for cleaning the hallways of buildings.
As a custodian, the BEST way for you to acquaint your men with this new procedure and to get them to use it is to

    A. wait until it has been tried out in another building and, if it is successful, put it into use in your building
    B. give each man a printed copy of the new procedure and set a deadline date by which each man is to read it and know it
    C. get your men together and explain the new procedure to them and how it will affect their work
    D. teach it to your best man and when he is familiar with it, ask him to teach it to the other men one at a time

19.____

20. Suppose that, as a custodian, you have finished *breaking in* a new employee. A few days later, you see the new man doing the job the wrong way.
You should

    A. immediately show the man what he is doing wrong and how to do it correctly
    B. assign him to some other work
    C. let your superior know that the new man cannot follow instructions
    D. say nothing because you may make the new man nervous

20.____

21. Suppose that a new type waxing machine is to be used in your building.
Of the following, the BEST way for you to teach your men how to use this machine is to

    A. give a talk on how to operate the machine
    B. demonstrate the operation and then have each man operate the machine under your supervision
    C. have the manufacturer give a talk on how to operate the machine
    D. give each man a set of carefully written instructions on how to operate the machine

21.____

22. When a custodian has to teach a man a new job, it would be MOST helpful for him to find out

    A. how long the man has been with the department and how long he plans to stay
    B. the man's dependability and willingness
    C. the man's past record of cooperation with other workers
    D. what the man already knows that will help him in learning the new job

23. When a new custodian comes on the job, it is LEAST important for him to know

    A. the location of the buildings in the unit
    B. how long the foremen have been there
    C. the names of the men who work there
    D. where the tools and equipment are kept

24. When you assign work to your men, it is usually BEST to

    A. give each man the same amount of work
    B. give the jobs that take the longest time to the senior men
    C. assign work to each man according to his ability
    D. let each man pick his own assignment

25. As a custodian, you will MOST likely be respected by your men if you

    A. keep your personnel records simple and clear
    B. offer them advice in solving their family problems
    C. leave it to them to decide how a job is to be done
    D. are fair and honest with them

KEY (CORRECT ANSWERS)

1. C
2. C
3. A
4. D
5. C

6. B
7. C
8. A
9. B
10. A

11. C
12. A
13. D
14. B
15. D

16. D
17. A
18. C
19. C
20. A

21. B
22. D
23. B
24. C
25. D

TEST 3

DIRECTIONS: Each question or incomplete statement is followed by several suggested answers or completions. Select the one that BEST answers the question or completes the statement. *PRINT THE LETTER OF THE CORRECT ANSWER IN THE SPACE AT THE RIGHT.*

1. Good public relations can be damaged by a custodian who treats tenants, fellow workers, friends, relatives, and the public with

    A. courtesy
    B. consideration
    C. contempt
    D. respect

    1.___

2. An office worker complains to a custodian that one of the cleaners broke off a branch of a plant which she kept on her desk and that she can identify the cleaner.
   The BEST thing for the custodian to do is to

    A. convince her that the plant will grow another branch eventually
    B. make the cleaner apologize and pay for a new plant out of his own pocket
    C. sympathize with the office worker and assure her that he will speak to the cleaner about it
    D. tell her not to bother him about her personal property

    2.___

3. When a new employee reports to a custodian on his first day on the job, the custodian SHOULD

    A. extend a hearty welcome and make the new employee feel welcome
    B. have the man sit and wait for a while before seeing him so that the employee realizes how busy the custodian is
    C. warn him of stern disciplinary action if he is late or absent excessively
    D. tell him he probably will have difficulty doing the work so that he doesn't become overconfident

    3.___

4. The one of the following subjects of a fire prevention training program which is MOST readily applied on the job is the

    A. elimination of fire hazards
    B. use of portable fire extinguishers
    C. knowledge of types of fires
    D. method of reporting fires

    4.___

5. A custodian who is a good supervisor will NOT

    A. tell his men what their jobs are and why they are important
    B. show his men how their jobs are to be done in the right way
    C. require some of the men to do their jobs in the presence of the supervisor demonstrating that they understand the job
    D. leave his men alone because they will always do their jobs correctly once they have received their instructions

    5.___

6. When a custodian sees a worker doing his job incorrectly, he should

    A. tell the worker to be more careful
    B. suspend the worker until he learns to do the job correctly
    C. tell the worker specifically how the job should be done
    D. scold the man

    6.___

7. An employee who is a good worker but is often late for work　　　　　　　　　　7._____

   A. is lazy and should be dismissed
   B. cannot tell time
   C. can have no excuse for being late more than once a month
   D. should be questioned by his supervisor to try to find out why he is late

8. When starting any disciplinary action, a custodian who is a good supervisor should　　　8._____

   A. show his annoyance by losing his temper
   B. be apologetic
   C. be sarcastic
   D. be firm and positive

9. The BEST way for a custodian to maintain good employee morale is to　　　　　　9._____

   A. avoid praising any one employee
   B. always have an alibi for his own mistakes
   C. encourage cliques by giving them information before giving it to other workers
   D. give adequate credit and praise when due

10. The BEST way for a custodian to tell if the night cleaners have done their work well is to check　　10._____

    A. on how much cleaning material has been used
    B. on how much waste paper was collected
    C. the building for cleanliness
    D. the floor mops to see if they are still wet

11. The one of the following which is the BEST reason for introducing a training program is that the　　11._____

    A. quality of work is above standard
    B. employees are all experienced
    C. accident rate is too high
    D. complaints are negligible

12. The FIRST step in training an inexperienced individual in a particular job is to　　　12._____

    A. put him to work and watch for mistakes
    B. put him to work and tell him to call for help if he needs it
    C. put him at ease and then find out what he knows about the work
    D. tell him to watch the least experienced worker on the job because the training is still fresh in his mind

13. As used in job analysis, the term *job breakdown* means　　　　　　　　　　13._____

    A. any equipment failure
    B. any failure on the part of the worker to complete the job
    C. dividing the job into a series of steps
    D. reducing the number of workers by 50 percent

14. In dealing with the public, a custodian should be

    A. indulgent
    B. courteous
    C. disagreeable
    D. unavailable

15. If a custodian sees a group of people in front of his building preparing to form a picket line, he should

    A. turn on a lawn sprinkler to spray the pickets
    B. order the pickets off the sidewalk in front of the building
    C. show the pickets he is sympathetic with their complaint against the city
    D. contact his supervisor immediately for instructions

16. When electric service in a public building is to be shut off from 10 A.M. Tuesday to 11:30 the next morning because a new electric feeder cable is being installed, the custodian should

    A. prepare a memo to all office supervisors in the building, notifying them of the situation, and deliver a copy to each office as soon as possible
    B. prepare a notice of the impending power stoppage and post it in the lobby early Tuesday morning
    C. tell the electrical contractor to notify the tenants when he is about to shut off the power
    D. discontinue elevator service at 10 A.M. on Tuesday as an indication to the tenants that the power supply is off

17. Time standards for cleaning are of value ONLY if

    A. a bonus is promised if the time standards are beaten
    B. the cleaners determine the methods and procedures to be used
    C. accompanied by a completely detailed description of the methods to be used
    D. a schematic diagram of the area is made available to the cleaners

18. Of the following, the one which is the LEAST important factor in deciding that additional training is necessary for the men you supervise is that

    A. the quality of work is below standard
    B. supplies are being wasted
    C. too much time is required to do specific jobs
    D. the absentee rate has declined

19. To promote proper safety practices in the operation of power tools and equipment, the custodian should emphasize in meetings with his staff that

    A. every accident can be prevented through proper safety regulations
    B. proper safety practices will probably make future safety meetings unnecessary
    C. when safety rules are followed, tools and equipment will work better
    D. safety rules are based on past experience with the best methods of preventing accidents

20. As a custodian, a GOOD practical method to use in determining whether an employee is doing his job properly is to 20.____

    A. assume that if he asks no questions, he knows the work
    B. question him directly on details of the job
    C. inspect and follow-up the work which is assigned to him
    D. ask other employees how this employee is making out

21. If an employee continually asks how he should do his work, the custodian should 21.____

    A. dismiss him immediately
    B. pretend he does not hear him unless he persists
    C. explain the work carefully but encourage him to use his own judgment
    D. tell him not to ask so many questions

22. As a custodian, you have instructed an employee to wet mop a certain area. To be sure that the employee understands the instructions you have given him, you should 22.____

    A. ask him to repeat the instructions to you
    B. check with him after he has done the job
    C. watch him while he is doing the job
    D. repeat the instructions to the employee

23. As a custodian, one of your men disagrees with your evaluation of his work. Of the following, the BEST way to handle this situation would be to 23.____

    A. explain that you are in a better position to evaluate his work than he is
    B. tell him that since the other men are satisfied with your evaluation, he should accept their opinions
    C. explain the basis of your evaluation and discuss it with him
    D. refuse to discuss his complaint in order to maintain discipline

24. Of the following, the one which is NOT a purpose of a cleaning job breakdown is to 24.____

    A. eliminate unnecessary steps
    B. determine the type of floor wax to use
    C. rearrange the sequence of operations to save time
    D. combine steps or actions where practicable

25. The BEST method of making cleaning assignments in a large building is by means of 25.____

    A. daily rotation   B. specific assignment
    C. individual choice   D. chronological order

KEY (CORRECT ANSWERS)

1. C
2. C
3. A
4. A
5. D

6. C
7. D
8. D
9. D
10. C

11. C
12. C
13. C
14. B
15. D

16. A
17. C
18. D
19. D
20. C

21. C
22. A
23. C
24. B
25. B

EXAMINATION SECTION
TEST 1

DIRECTIONS: Each question or incomplete statement is followed by several suggested answers or completions. Select the one that BEST answers the question or completes the statement. *PRINT THE LETTER OF THE CORRECT ANSWER IN THE SPACE AT THE RIGHT.*

1. A custodian was given a booklet that showed a new work method that could save time. He didn't tell his men because he thought that they would get the booklet anyway. For the custodian to have acted like this is a

    A. *good* idea, because he saves the time and bother of talking to the men
    B. *bad* idea, because he should make sure his men know about better work methods
    C. *good* idea, because the men would rather read about it themselves
    D. *bad* idea, because a supervisor should always show his men every memo he gets from higher authority

    1.____

2. A custodian found it necessary to discipline two subordinates. One man had been operating his equipment in a wrong way, while the other man came to work late for three days in a row. The supervisor decided to talk to both men together.
For the custodian to deal with the problems in this way is a

    A. *good* idea, because each man will learn about the difficulties of the other person and how to solve such difficulties
    B. *bad* idea, because the supervisor should wait until he can bring a larger group together and save time in discussing such questions
    C. *good* idea, because he will be able to get the men to see that their problems are related
    D. *bad* idea, because he should meet with each man separately and give him his full attention

    2.____

3. A custodian should try to make his men feel their jobs are important in order to

    A. get the men to say good things about their supervisor to his own superior
    B. get the men to think in terms of advancing to better jobs
    C. let higher management in the agency know that the supervisor is efficient
    D. help the men to be able to work more efficiently and enthusiastically

    3.____

4. A custodian should know approximately how long it takes to do a particular kind of job CHIEFLY because he

    A. will know how much time to take if he has to do it himself
    B. will be able to tell his men to do it even faster
    C. can judge the performance of the person doing the job
    D. can retrain experienced employees in better work habits

    4.____

5. Custodians often get their employees' opinions about better work methods because

    A. the men will know that they are respected
    B. the men would otherwise lose all their confidence in the supervisor
    C. the supervisor might find in this way a good suggestion he could use
    D. this is the best method for improvement of work methods

    5.____

6. Right after you have trained your subordinates in doing a new job, you find that they seem to be doing all right, but that it will take them several days to finish. You also have several groups of men working at other locations. The MOST efficient way for you to make sure that the men continue doing the new job properly is to

    A. stay on that job with the men until it is finished, just in case trouble develops
    B. visit the men every half hour until the job is done
    C. stay away from their job that day, and visit the men the next day to ask them if they had any problems
    D. visit the men a few times each day until they finish the new job

7. Assume that one of your new employees is older than you are. You also think that he may be hard to get along with because he is older than you.
   The BEST way for you to avoid any problems with the older worker is for you to

    A. *lay down the law* immediately and tell the man he better not cause you any trouble
    B. treat the man just the way you would any other worker
    C. always ask the older worker for advice in the presence of all the men
    D. ignore the man entirely until he realizes that you are the boss

8. Assume you have tried a new method suggested by one of your employees, and find that it is easier and cheaper than the method you had been using.
   The proper thing for you to do NEXT is to

    A. say nothing to anyone, but train your men to use the new method
    B. train your men to use the new method and tell your crew that you got the idea from one of the men
    C. continue using the old method, because a supervisor should not use suggestions of his men
    D. have your crew learn the new method and take credit for the idea since you are the boss

9. Suppose you are a custodian and your superior tells you that the way your men are doing a certain procedure is wrong and that you should re-train your men as soon as possible. When you begin to re-train the men, the FIRST thing you should do is

    A. tell your men that a wrong procedure had been used and that a new method must be learned as a result
    B. train your employees in the new method with no explanation, since you are the boss
    C. tell the crew that your superior has just decided that everyone should learn a new method
    D. tell the crew that your superior says your method is wrong, but that you don't agree with this

10. It is *bad* practice to criticize a man in front of the other men because

    A. people will think you are too strict
    B. it is annoying to anyone who walks by
    C. it is embarrassing to the man concerned
    D. it will antagonize the other men

11. A custodian decides not to put his two best men on a work detail because he knows that 11.____
    they won't like it.
    For the custodian to make the work assignment this way is a

    A. *good* idea, because it is only fair to give your best men a break once in a while
    B. *bad* idea, because you should treat all of your men fairly and not show favoritism
    C. *good* idea, because you save the strength of these men for another job
    D. *bad* idea, because more of the men should be exempted from the assignment

12. Suppose you are a custodian and you find it inconvenient to obey an established proce- 12.____
    dure set by your agency. You think another procedure would be better.
    The BEST thing to do FIRST about this procedure that you don't like is for you to

    A. obey the procedure even if you don't want to, and suggest your idea to your own supervisor
    B. disregard the procedure because a supervisor is supposed to have some privileges
    C. follow the procedure some of the time, but ignore it when the men aren't watching
    D. organize a group of other supervisors to get the procedure changed

13. A custodian estimated that it would take his crew one workday per week to do a certain 13.____
    job each week. However, after a month he noticed that the job averaged two-and-a-half days a week, and this delayed other jobs that had to be done.
    The FIRST thing that the custodian should do in this case is to

    A. call his men together and warn them that they will get a poor work evaluation if they don't work harder
    B. talk to each man personally, asking him to work harder on the job
    C. go back and study the maintenance job by himself, to see if more men should be assigned to the job
    D. write his boss a report describing in detail how much time it is taking the men to do the job

14. An employee complains to you that some of his work assignments are too difficult to do 14.____
    alone.
    Which of the following is the BEST way for you to handle this complaint?

    A. Go with him to see exactly what he does and why he finds it so difficult.
    B. Politely tell the man that he has to do the job or be brought up on charges.
    C. Tell the man to send his complaint to the head of your agency.
    D. Sympathize with the man and give him easier jobs.

15. The BEST way for a custodian to keep control of his work assignments is to 15.____

    A. ask the men to report to him immediately when their jobs are finished
    B. walk around the buildings once a week, and get a first-hand view of what is being done
    C. keep his ears open for problems and complaints, but leave the men alone to do the work
    D. write up a work schedule, and check it periodically against the actual work done

4 (#1)

16. A custodian made a work schedule for his men. At the bottom of it he wrote, *No changes or exceptions will be made in this schedule for any reason.*
For the custodian to have made this statement is

   A. *good,* because the men will respect the custodian for his attitude
   B. *bad,* because there are emergencies and special situations that occur
   C. *good,* because each man will know exactly what is expected of him
   D. *bad,* because the men should expect that no changes will ever be made in the work schedule without written permission

16.____

17. Which one of the following would NOT be a result of a well-planned work schedule?
The schedule

   A. makes efficient use of the time of the staff
   B. acts as a checklist for an important job that might be left out
   C. will give an idea of the work to a substitute supervisor
   D. shows at a glance who the best men are

17.____

18. A new piece of equipment you have ordered is delivered. You are familiar with it but the men under you, who will use it, do not know the equipment.
Of the following methods, which is the BEST to take in explaining to them how to operate this equipment?

   A. Ask the men to watch other crews using the equipment
   B. Show one reliable man how to operate the equipment and ask him to teach the other men
   C. Ask the men to read the instructions in the manual for the equipment
   D. Call the men together and show them how to operate the equipment

18.____

19. One custodian assigns work to his men by calling his crew together each week and describing what has to be done that week. He then tells them to arrange individual assignments among themselves and to work as a team during the week.
This method of scheduling work is a

   A. *good* idea, because this guarantees that the men will work together
   B. *bad* idea, because responsibility for doing the job is poorly fixed
   C. *good* idea, because the men will finish the job in less tirae working together
   D. *bad* idea, because the supervisor should always stay with his men

19.____

20. Suppose that a custodial assistant came to the custodian with a problem concerning his assignment.
For the custodian to listen to this problem is a

   A. *good* idea, because a supervisor should always take time off to talk when one of his men wants to talk
   B. *bad* idea, because the supervisor should not be bothered during the work day
   C. *good* idea, because it's the job of the supervisor to deal with problems of job assignment
   D. *bad* idea, because the employee could start annoying the supervisor with all sorts of problems

20.____

21. Suppose that on the previous afternoon you were looking for an experienced employee in order to give him an emergency job and he was missing from his job location. The next morning he tells you that he got sick suddenly and had to go home, but couldn't tell you since you weren't around. He has never done this before.
    What should you do?

    A. Tell the man he is excused and that in such circumstances he did the wisest thing.
    B. Bring the man up on charges because, whatever he says, he could still have notified you.
    C. Have the man examined by a doctor to see if he really was sick the day before
    D. Explain to the man that he should make every effort to tell or to get a message to you if he must leave

22. An employee had a grievance and went to the custodian about it. The employee wasn't satisfied with the way the custodian tried to help him, and told him so. Yet the custodian had done everything he could under the circumstances.
    The PROPER action for the supervisor to take at this time is to

    A. politely tell the employee that there is nothing more for the custodian to do about the problem
    B. let the employee know how he can bring his complaint to a higher authority
    C. tell the employee that he must solve the problem on his own, since he didn't want to follow the custodian's advice
    D. suggest to the employee that he ask another supervisor for assistance

23. In which of the following situations is it BEST to give your men spoken rather than written orders?

    A. You want your men to have a record of the instructions.
    B. Spoken instructions are less likely to be forgotten.
    C. An emergency situation has arisen in which there is no time to write up instructions.
    D. There are instructions on time and leave regulations which are complicated.

24. One of your employees tells you that a week ago he had a small accident on the job, but he didn't bother telling you because he was able to continue working.
    For the employee not to have told the custodian about the accident was

    A. *good,* because the accident was a small one
    B. *bad,* because all accidents should be reported, no matter how small
    C. *good,* because the custodian should be bothered only for important matters
    D. *bad,* because having an accident is one way to get excused for the day

25. For a custodian to deal with each of his subordinates in exactly the same manner is

    A. *poor,* because each man presents a different problem and there is no other way of handling all problems
    B. *good,* because once a problem is handled with one man, he can handle another man with the same problem
    C. *poor,* because the men will resent it if they are not handled each in a better way than others
    D. *good,* because this assures fair and impartial treatment of each subordinate

KEY (CORRECT ANSWERS)

1.	B	11.	B
2.	D	12.	A
3.	D	13.	C
4.	C	14.	A
5.	C	15.	D
6.	D	16.	B
7.	B	17.	D
8.	B	18.	D
9.	A	19.	B
10.	C	20.	C

21. D
22. B
23. C
24. B
25. A

TEST 2

DIRECTIONS: Each question or incomplete statement is followed by several suggested answers or completions. Select the one that BEST answers the question or completes the statement. *PRINT THE LETTER OF THE CORRECT ANSWER IN THE SPACE AT THE RIGHT.*

1. One day a custodial assistant said to the custodian, *I can get a tile cleaner that is as good as the stuff we use, and for less money, because my brother is a building contractor. How about it?*
   The CORRECT way for the custodian to handle this situation is for him to

   A. thank the assistant, but tell him that individual workers cannot buy their own cleaning material for project use
   B. tell the assistant that no one has any right to start interfering in the buying procedures of the authority
   C. go along with the assistant and buy the cleaner from his brother, because it might save money for the authority
   D. tell the assistant to have his brother contact the project manager

   1.____

2. A new custodial assistant under your supervision is waxing a floor for the first time. While the job seems to be going along well, he is not doing it quite the way you asked him to do it and so is taking longer than he should. Which of the following is the BEST action for you to take under these conditions?

   A. Leave him to finish the job and go on to the next one
   B. Interrupt him and tell him to do the job the way he was taught
   C. Tell him he is doing well but that he should do better
   D. Explain to him why your way is faster and tell him to try it

   2.____

3. The easiest way for a custodian to find out how many supplies are available is to

   A. look at last year's figures
   B. keep an up-to-date inventory
   C. ask one of the men to let you know
   D. check the availability when he uses a special item

   3.____

4. Of the following, the MOST likely result of a report that has been planned well is that it will

   A. explain, in detail, general procedures of supervision
   B. be read by most of the top officials of the department
   C. have some award-winning suggestions
   D. state the facts in a clear, orderly way

   4.____

5. It is better to make a written report, instead of a face-to-face report, when

   A. you expect your superior to have questions about what is in the report right away
   B. your superior wants to know about your work immediately
   C. the report is very short
   D. you will have to give your report to many people in different locations

   5.____

6. Of the following, the MOST important fact a custodian should include in an accident report is

   A. the name of the insurance company of the injured person
   B. cost to the city of the accident
   C. name and address of the injured person
   D. your idea for preventing such an accident in the future

7. Making an outline of the contents of a long report, before writing the report, is often a good idea. The advantage is that

   A. you can file an outline to refer to it in the future
   B. your supervisor can see it and know that you are working on the report
   C. you can make the outline a part of your report
   D. it will help you in writing the report

8. Of the following, the MOST important reason for the custodian's making detailed reports in all accidents is to

   A. have a record of who is at fault in case lawsuits should result
   B. be better able to estimate the cost of the accident
   C. reduce the number of compensation claims
   D. determine the cause of the accident and prevent future accidents

9. A custodian's written instructions to his staff on the subject of security in public buildings should include instructions to

   A. exclude the public at all times
   B. admit the public at all times
   C. admit the public only if they are neat and well-dressed
   D. admit the public during specified hours

10. The key figure in any custodial safety program is the

    A. building custodian   B. cleaner
    C. operating engineer   D. commissioner

11. A supervisor should know the equipment used in his work well enough to

    A. make any repairs which might be needed
    B. know what parts to remove in case of breakdown
    C. anticipate any reasonable possibility of a breakdown
    D. know all the lubricants specified by the manufacturer

12. The PRIMARY responsibility of a building custodian is to

    A. make friends of all subordinates
    B. search for new methods of doing the work
    C. win the respect of his superior
    D. get the work done properly within a reasonable time

13. If the directions given by your superior are not clear, the BEST thing for you to do is to

A. ask to have the directions repeated and clarified
B. proceed to do the work taking a chance on doing the right thing
C. do nothing until some later time when you can find out exactly what is wanted
D. ask one of the other men in your crew what he would do under the circumstances

14. Of the following procedures concerning grievances of subordinate personnel, the custodian-engineer should maintain an attitude on

    A. paying little attention to little grievances
    B. being very alert to grievances and make adjustments in existing conditions to appease all personnel
    C. knowing the most frequent causes of grievances and strive to prevent them from arising
    D. maintaining firm discipline of a nature that *smooths out* all grievances

15. Of the following, the BEST course of action to take to settle a dispute or conflict between two employees is to

    A. insist that the two employees settle the case between themselves
    B. call in each one separately and, after hearing their cases presented, decide the issue
    C. bring both in for a conference at the same time and make the decision in their presence
    D. have both present their points of view and arguments in written memoranda and on this basis make your decision

16. If, as a custodian-engineer, you discover an error in your report submitted to the main office, you should

    A. do nothing, since it is possible that one error will have little effect on the total report
    B. wait until the error is discovered in the main office and then offer to work overtime to correct it
    C. go directly to the supervisor in the main office after working hours and ask him unofficially to correct the error
    D. notify the main office immediately so that the error can be corrected, if necessary

17. There are a considerable number of forms and reports to be submitted on schedule by the custodian-engineer. The ADVISABLE method of accomplishing this duty is to

    A. fill out the reports at odd times during the days when you have free time
    B. schedule a definite period of the work week for completing these forms and reports
    C. assign your foreman or cleaner to handle all these forms for you and to have them available on time
    D. classify or group the forms and reports and fill out only one of each group and refer the other forms or reports to the ones completed

18. A custodian-engineer can BEST evaluate the quality of work performed by custodial personnel by

    A. periodic inspection of the building's cleanliness
    B. studying the time records of personnel
    C. reviewing the building cleaning expenditures
    D. analyzing complaints of building occupants

19. Assume that you are the custodian-engineer and one of your employees wants to talk with you about a grievance. Of the following actions, the LEAST desirable action for you to take is to

    A. listen sympathetically
    B. conduct the discussion openly in the presence of the workforce
    C. try to get his point of view
    D. endeavor to obtain all the facts

20. Of the following factors, the one which is LEAST important in evaluating an employee and his work is his

    A. dependability
    B. quantity of work
    C. quality of work
    D. education and training

21. Supervision of a group of people engaged in building cleaning operations should NOT include supervision of

    A. time spent in cleaning operations
    B. utilization of official rest and lunch periods
    C. cleaning methods
    D. materials used for various cleaning jobs

22. Of the following methods, the BEST one to utilize in assigning custodial personnel to clean a multi-floor school building is to

    A. allow the cleaners to pick their rooms or area assignments out of a hat
    B. have the supervisor make specific room or area assignments to each cleaner separately
    C. rotate room and area assignments daily according to a chart posted on the bulletin board
    D. let a different member of the group make the room or area assignments each week

23. Assume that you are the custodian-engineer and that you have discovered a bottle of liquor in one of your employees' locker. The BEST course of action to take is to

    A. fire him immediately
    B. explain to him that liquor should not be brought into a school building and that a repetition may result in disciplinary action
    C. suspend him until the end of the week and take him back only on a probational basis
    D. assemble the staff and tell them they are all equally guilty for not having reported the matter to you

24. Of the following items, the one which is the LEAST important in the preparation of a report is that the report

    A. is brief, but to the point
    B. uses the prescribed form if there is one
    C. contains extra copies
    D. is accurate

25. In order to have building employees willing to follow standardized cleaning and mainte- 25._____
nance procedures, the supervisor must be prepared to
- A. work alongside the employees
- B. demonstrate the reasonableness of the procedures
- C. offer incentive pay for their utilization
- D. allow the employees the free use of the time saved by their adoption

---

KEY (CORRECT ANSWERS)

1.	A	11.	C
2.	D	12.	D
3.	B	13.	A
4.	B	14.	C
5.	D	15.	C
6.	C	16.	D
7.	D	17.	B
8.	D	18.	A
9.	D	19.	B
10.	A	20.	D

21.	B
22.	B
23.	B
24.	C
25.	B

PREPARING WRITTEN MATERIAL
EXAMINATION SECTION
TEST 1

DIRECTIONS: Each question consists of a sentence which may or may not be an example of good English usage. Examine each sentence, considering grammar, punctuation, spelling, capitalization, and awkwardness. Then choose the correct statement about it from the four choices below it. If the English usage in the sentence given is better than any of the changes suggested in choices B, C, or D, pick choice A. (Do not pick a choice that will change the meaning of the sentence.) *PRINT THE LETTER OF THE CORRECT ANSWER IN THE SPACE AT THE RIGHT.*

1. We attended a staff conference on Wednesday the new safety and fire rules were discussed.
    A. This is an example of acceptable writing.
    B. The words "safety," "fire," and "rules" should begin with capital letters.
    C. There should be a comma after the word "Wednesday."
    D. There should be a period after the word "Wednesday" and the word "the" should begin with a capital letter.

1.____

2. Neither the dictionary or the telephone directory could be found in the office library.
    A. This is an example of acceptable writing.
    B. The word "or" should be changed to "nor."
    C. The word "library" should be spelled "libery."
    D. The word "neither" should be changed to "either."

2.____

3. The report would have been typed correctly if the typist could read the draft.
    A. This is an example of acceptable writing.
    B. The word "would" should be removed.
    C. The word "have" should be inserted after the word "could."
    D. The word "correctly" should be changed to "correct."

3.____

4. The supervisor brought the reports and forms to an employees desk.
    A. This is an example of acceptable writing.
    B. The word "brought" should be changed to "took."
    C. There should be a comma after the word "reports" and a comma after the word "forms."
    D. The word "employees" should be spelled "employee's."

4.____

5. It's important for all the office personnel to submit their vacation schedules on time.
    A. This is an example of acceptable writing.
    B. The word "It's" should be spelled "Its."
    C. The word "their" should be spelled "they're."
    D. The word "personnel" should be spelled "personal."

5.____

101

6. The report, along with the accompanying documents, were submitted for review.
   A. This is an example of acceptable writing.
   B. The words "were submitted" should be changed to "was submitted."
   C. The word "accompanying" should be spelled "accompaning."
   D. The comma after the word "report" should be taken out.

   6.____

7. If others must use your files, be certain that they understand how the system works, but insist that you do all the filing and refiling.
   A. This is an example of acceptable writing.
   B. There should be a period after the word "works," and the word "but" should start a new sentence.
   C. The words "filing" and "refiling" should be spelled "fileing" and "refileing."
   D. There should be a comma after the word "but."

   7.____

8. The appeal was not considered because of its late arrival.
   A. This is an example of acceptable writing.
   B. The word "its" should be changed to "it's."
   C. The word "its" should be changed to "the."
   D. The words "late arrival" should be changed to "arrival late."

   8.____

9. The letter must be read carefuly to determine under which subject it should be filed.
   A. This is an example of acceptable writing.
   B. The word "under" should be changed to "at."
   C. The word "determine" should be spelled "determin."
   D. The word "carefuly" should be spelled "carefully."

   9.____

10. He showed potential as an office manager, but he lacked skill in delegating work.
    A. This is an example of acceptable writing.
    B. The word "delegating" should be spelled "delagating."
    C. The word "potential" should be spelled "potencial."
    D. The words "he lacked" should be changed to "was lacking."

    10.____

KEY (CORRECT ANSWERS)

1.	D	6.	B
2.	B	7.	A
3.	C	8.	A
4.	D	9.	D
5.	A	10.	A

TEST 2

DIRECTIONS: Each question consists of a sentence which may or may not be an example of good English usage. Examine each sentence, considering grammar, punctuation, spelling, capitalization, and awkwardness. Then choose the correct statement about it from the four choices below it. If the English usage in the sentence given is better than any of the changes suggested in choices B, C, or D, pick choice A. (Do not pick a choice that will change the meaning of the sentence.) *PRINT THE LETTER OF THE CORRECT ANSWER IN THE SPACE AT THE RIGHT.*

1. The supervisor wants that all staff members report to the office at 9:00 A.M.
   A. This is an example of acceptable writing.
   B. The word "that" should be removed and the word "to" should be inserted after the word "members."
   C. There should be a comma after the word "wants" and a comma after the word "office."
   D. The word "wants" should be changed to "want" and the word "shall" should be inserted after the word "members."

   1.____

2. Every morning the clerk opens the office mail and distributes it.
   A. This is an example of acceptable writing.
   B. The word "opens" should be changed to "open."
   C. The word "mail" should be changed to "letters."
   D. The word "it" should be changed to "them."

   2.____

3. The secretary typed more fast on a desktop computer than on a laptop computer.
   A. This is an example of acceptable writing.
   B. The words "more fast" should be changed to "faster."
   C. There should be a comma after the words "desktop computer."
   D. The word "than" should be changed to "then."

   3.____

4. The new stenographer needed a desk a computer, a chair and a blotter.
   A. This is an example of acceptable writing.
   B. The word "blotter" should be spelled "blodder."
   C. The word "stenographer" should begin with a capital letter.
   D. There should be a comma after the word "desk."

   4.____

5. The recruiting officer said, "There are many different goverment jobs available."
   A. This is an example of acceptable writing.
   B. The word "There" should not be capitalized.
   C. The word "government" should be spelled "government."
   D. The comma after the word "said" should be removed.

   5.____

6. He can recommend a mechanic whose work is reliable.
   A. This is an example of acceptable writing.
   B. The word "reliable" should be spelled "relyable."
   C. The word "whose" should be spelled "who's."
   D. The word "mechanic should be spelled "mecanic."

   6.____

103

7. She typed quickly; like someone who had not a moment to lose.
   A. This is an example of acceptable writing.
   B. The word "not" should be removed.
   C. The semicolon should be changed to a comma.
   D. The word "quickly" should be placed before instead of after the word "typed."

8. She insisted that she had to much work to do.
   A. This is an example of acceptable writing.
   B. The word "insisted" should be spelled "incisted."
   C. The word "to" used in front of "much" should be spelled "too."
   D. The word "do" should be changed to "be done."

9. He excepted praise from his supervisor for a job well done.
   A. This is an example of acceptable writing.
   B. The word "excepted" should be spelled "accepted."
   C. The order of the words "well done" should be changed to "done well."
   D. There should be a comma after the word "supervisor."

10. What appears to be intentional errors in grammar occur several times in the passage.
    A. This is an example of acceptable writing.
    B. The word "occur" should be spelled "occurr."
    C. The word "appears" should be changed to "appear."
    D. The phrase "several times" should be changed to "from time to time."

KEY (CORRECT ANSWERS)

1. B
2. A
3. B
4. D
5. C
6. A
7. C
8. C
9. B
10. C

TEST 3

DIRECTIONS: Each question consists of a sentence which may or may not be an example of good English usage. Examine each sentence, considering grammar, punctuation, spelling, capitalization, and awkwardness. Then choose the correct statement about it from the four choices below it. If the English usage in the sentence given is better than any of the changes suggested in choices B, C, or D, pick choice A. (Do not pick a choice that will change the meaning of the sentence.) *PRINT THE LETTER OF THE CORRECT ANSWER IN THE SPACE AT THE RIGHT.*

1. The clerk could have completed the assignment on time if he knows where these materials were located.
    A. This is an example of acceptable writing.
    B. The word "knows" should be replaced by "had known."
    C. The word "were" should be replaced by "had been."
    D. The words "where these materials were located" should be replaced by "the location of these materials."

2. All employees should be given safety training. Not just those who accidents.
    A. This is an example of acceptable writing.
    B. The period after the word "training" should be changed to a colon.
    C. The period after the word "training" should be changed to a semicolon, and the first letter of the word "Not" should be changed to a small "n."
    D. The period after the word "training" should be changed to a comma, and the first letter of the word "Not" should be changed to a small "n."

3. This proposal is designed to promote employee awareness of the suggestion program, to encourage employee participation in the program, and to increase the number of suggestions submitted.
    A. This is an example of acceptable writing.
    B. The word "proposal" should be spelled "proposal."
    C. The words "to increase the number of suggestions submitted" should be changed to "an increase in the number of suggestions is expected."
    D. The word "promote" should be changed to "enhance" and the word "increase" should be changed to "add to."

4. The introduction of inovative managerial techniques should be preceded by careful analysis of the specific circumstances and conditions in each department.
    A. This is an example of acceptable writing.
    B. The word "technique" should be spelled "techneques."
    C. The word "inovative" should be spelled "innovative."
    D. A comma should be placed after the word "circumstances" and after the word "conditions."

5. This occurrence indicates that such criticism embarrasses him. 5.____
   A. This is an example of acceptable writing.
   B. The word "occurrence" should be spelled "occurence."
   C. The word "criticism" should be spelled "critisism.
   D. The word "embarrasses" should be spelled "embarasses.

KEY (CORRECT ANSWERS)

1. B
2. D
3. A
4. C
5. A

PREPARING WRITTEN MATERIAL
EXAMINATION SECTION
TEST 1

DIRECTIONS: Each of Questions 1 through 5 consists of a sentence which may or may not be an example of good formal English usage. Examine each sentence, considering grammar, punctuation, spelling, capitalization, and awkwardness. Then choose the correct statement about it from the four options below it. If the English usage in the sentence given is better than any of the changes suggested in options B, C, or D, pick option A. (Do not pick an option that will change the meaning of the sentence.) *PRINT THE LETTER OF THE CORRECT ANSWER IN THE SPACE AT THE RIGHT.*

1. I don't know who could possibly of broken it. 1.____
   A. This is an example of good formal English usage.
   B. The word "who" should be replaced by the word "whom."
   C. The word "of" should be replaced by the word "have."
   D. The word "broken" should be replaced by the word "broke."

2. Telephoning is easier than to write. 2.____
   A. This is an example of good formal English usage.
   B. The word "telephoning" should be spelled "telephoneing."
   C. The word "than" should be replaced by the word "then."
   D. The words "to write" should be replaced by the word "writing."

3. The two operators who have been assigned to these consoles are on vacation. 3.____
   A. This is an example of good formal English usage.
   B. A comma should be placed after the word "operators."
   C. The word "who" should be replaced by the word "whom."
   D. The word "are" should be replaced by the word "is."

4. You were suppose to teach me how to operate a plugboard. 4.____
   A. This is an example of good formal English usage.
   B. The word "were" should be replaced by the word "was."
   C. The word "suppose" should be replaced by the word "supposed."
   D. The word "teach" should be replaced by the word "learn."

5. If you had taken my advice; you would have spoken with him. 5.____
   A. This is an example of good formal English usage.
   B. The word "advice" should be spelled "advise."
   C. The words "had taken" should be replaced by the word "take."
   D. The semicolon should be changed to a comma.

KEY (CORRECT ANSWERS)

1. C
2. D
3. A
4. C
5. D

TEST 2

DIRECTIONS: Select the correct answer. *PRINT THE LETTER OF THE CORRECT ANSWER IN THE SPACE AT THE RIGHT.*

1. The one of the following sentences which is MOST acceptable from the viewpoint of correct grammatical usage is: 1.____
    A. I do not know which action will have worser results.
    B. He should of known better.
    C. Both the officer on the scene, and his immediate supervisor, is charged with the responsibility.
    D. An officer must have initiative because his supervisor will not always be available to answer questions.

2. The one of the following sentences which is MOST acceptable from the viewpoint of correct grammatical usage is: 2.____
    A. Of all the officers available, the better one for the job will be picked.
    B. Strict orders were given to all the officers, except he.
    C. Study of the law will enable you to perform your duties more efficiently.
    D. It seems to me that you was wrong in failing to search the two men.

3. The one of the following sentences which does NOT contain a misspelled word is: 3.____
    A. The duties you will perform are similar to the duties of a patrolman.
    B. Officers must be constantly alert to sieze the initiative.
    C. Officers in this organization are not entitled to special privileges.
    D. Any changes in procedure will be announced publically.

4. The one of the following sentences which does NOT contain a misspelled word is: 4.____
    A. It will be to your advantage to keep your firearm in good working condition.
    B. There are approximately fourty men on sick leave.
    C. Your first duty will be to pursuade the person to obey the law.
    D. Fires often begin in flameable material kept in lockers.

5. The one of the following sentences which does NOT contain a misspelled word is: 5.____
    A. Offices are not required to perform technical maintenance.
    B. He violated the regulations on two occasions.
    C. Every employee will be held responable for errors.
    D. This was his nineth absence in a year.

KEY (CORRECT ANSWERS)

1. D
2. C
3. C
4. A
5. B

TEST 3

DIRECTIONS: Select the correct answer. *PRINT THE LETTER OF THE CORRECT ANSWER IN THE SPACE AT THE RIGHT.*

1. You are answering a letter that was written on the letterhead of the ABC Company and signed by James H. Wood, Treasurer.
   What is usually considered to be the correct salutation to use in your reply?
   A. Dear ABC Company:
   B. Dear Sirs:
   C. Dear Mr. Wood:
   D. Dear Mr. Treasurer:

   1.____

2. Assume that one of your duties is to handle routine letters of inquiry from the public.
   The one of the following which is usually considered to be MOST desirable in replying to such a letter is a
   A. detailed answer handwritten on the original letter of inquiry
   B. phone call, since you can cover details more easily over the phone than in a letter
   C. short letter giving the specific information requested
   D. long letter discussing all possible aspects of the question raised

   2.____

3. The CHIEF reason for dividing a letter into paragraphs is to
   A. make the message clear to the reader by starting a new paragraph for each new topic
   B. make a short letter occupy as much of the page as possible
   C. keep the reader's attention by providing a pause from time to time
   D. make the letter look neat and businesslike

   3.____

4. Your superior has asked you to send an e-mail from your agency to a government agency in another city. He has written out the message and has indicated the name of the government agency.
   When you dictate the message to your secretary, which of the following items that your superior has NOT mentioned must you be sure to include?
   A. Today's date
   B. The full address of the government agency
   C. A polite opening such as "Dear Sirs"
   D. A final sentence such as "We would appreciate hearing from your agency in reply as soon as is convenient for you"

   4.____

5. The one of the following sentences which is grammatically preferable to the others is:
   A. Our engineers will go over your blueprints so that you may have no problems in construction.
   B. For a long time he had been arguing that we, not he, are to blame for the confusion.
   C. I worked on this automobile for two hours and still cannot find out what is wrong with it.
   D. Accustomed to all kinds of hardships, fatigue seldom bothers veteran policemen.

   5.____

KEY (CORRECT ANSWERS)

1. C
2. C
3. A
4. B
5. A

TEST 4

DIRECTIONS: Select the correct answer. *PRINT THE LETTER OF THE CORRECT ANSWER IN THE SPACE AT THE RIGHT.*

1. Suppose that an applicant for a job as snow laborer presents a letter from a former employer stating: "John Smith has a pleasing manner and never got into an argument with his fellow employees. He was never late or absent." This letter
    A. indicates that with some training Smith will make a good snow gang boss
    B. presents no definite evidence of Smith's ability to do snow work
    C. proves definitely that Smith has never done any snow work before
    D. proves definitely that Smith will do better than average work as a snow laborer

    1.____

2. Suppose you must write a letter to a local organization in your section refusing a request in connection with collection of their refuse.
   You should start the letter by
    A. explaining in detail the consideration you gave the request
    B. praising the organization for its service to the community
    C. quoting the regulation which forbids granting the request
    D. stating your regret that the request cannot be granted

    2.____

3. Suppose a citizen writes in for information as to whether or not he may sweep refuse into the gutter. A Sanitation officer answers as follows:
   Dear Sir:
      No person is permitted to litter, sweep, throw or cast, or direct, suffer or permit any person under his control to litter, sweep, throw or cast any ashes, garbage, paper, dust, or other rubbish or refuse into any public street or place, vacant lot, air shaft, areaway, backyard or court.
                           Very truly yours,
                           John Doe
   This letter is *poorly* written CHIEFLY because
    A. the opening is not indented   B. the thought is not clear
    C. the tone is too formal and cold   D. there are too many commas used

    3.____

4. A section of a disciplinary report written by a Sanitation officer states: "It is requested that subject Sanitation man be advised that his future activities be directed towards reducing his recurrent tardiness else disciplinary action will be initiated which may result in summary discharge."
   This section of the report is *poorly* written MAINLY because
    A. at least one word is misspelled   B. it is not simply expressed
    C. more than one idea is expressed   D. the purpose is not stated

    4.____

5. A section of a disciplinary report written by an officer states: "He comes in late. He takes too much time for lunch. He is lazy. I recommend his services be dispensed with."
   This section of the report is *poorly* written MAINLY because
    A. it ends with a preposition   B. it is not well organized
    C. no supporting facts are stated   D. the sentences are too simple

    5.____

KEY (CORRECT ANSWERS)

1. B
2. D
3. C
4. B
5. C

PREPARING WRITTEN MATERIAL

PARAGRAPH REARRANGEMENT
COMMENTARY

The sentences that follow are in scrambled order. You are to rearrange them in proper order and indicate the letter choice containing the correct answer at the space at the right.

Each group of sentences in this section is actually a paragraph presented in scrambled order. Each sentence in the group has a place in that paragraph; no sentence is to be left out. You are to read each group of sentences and decide upon the best order in which to put the sentences so as to form a well-organized paragraph.

The questions in this section measure the ability to solve a problem when all the facts relevant to its solution are not given.

More specifically, certain positions of responsibility and authority require the employee to discover connection between events sometimes, apparently, unrelated. In order to do this, the employee will find it necessary to correctly infer that unspecified events have probably occurred or are likely to occur. This ability becomes especially important when action must be taken on incomplete information.

Accordingly, these questions require competitors to choose among several suggested alternatives, each of which presents a different sequential arrangement of the events. Competitors must choose the MOST logical of the suggested sequences.

In order to do so, they may be required to draw on general knowledge to infer missing concepts or events that are essential to sequencing the given events. Competitors should be careful to infer only what is essential to the sequence. The plausibility of the wrong alternatives will always require the inclusion of unlikely events or of additional chains of events which are NOT essential to sequencing the given events.

It's very important to remember that you are looking for the best of the four possible choices, and that the best choice of all may not even be one of the answers you're given to choose from.

There is no one right way to solve these problems. Many people have found it helpful to first write out the order of the sentences, as they would have arranged them, on their scrap paper before looking at the possible answers. If their optimum answer is there, this can save them some time. If it isn't, this method can still give insight into solving the problem. Others find it most helpful to just go through each of the possible choices, contrasting each as they go along. You should use whatever method feels comfortable and works for you.

While most of these types of questions are not that difficult, we've added a higher percentage of the difficult type, just to give you more practice. Usually there are only one or two questions on this section that contain such subtle distinctions that you're unable to answer confidently. And you then may find yourself stuck deciding between two possible choices, neither of which you're sure about.

PREPARING WRITTEN MATERIAL
PARAGRAPH REARRANGEMENT
EXAMINATION SECTION
TEST 1

DIRECTIONS: The following groups of sentences need to be arranged in an order that makes sense. Select the letter preceding the sequence that represents the best sentence order. *PRINT THE LETTER OF THE CORRECT ANSWER IN THE SPACE AT THE RIGHT.*

1.
   I. The ostrich egg shell's legendary toughness makes it an excellent substitute for certain types of dishes or dinnerware, and in parts of Africa ostrich shells are cut and decorated for use as containers for water.
   II. Since prehistoric times, people have used the enormous egg of the ostrich as a part of their diet, a practice which has required much patience and hard work—to hard boil an ostrich egg takes about four hours.
   III. Opening the egg's shell, which is rock hard and nearly an inch thick, requires heavy tools, such as a saw or chisel; from inside, a baby ostrich must use a hornlike projection on its beak as a miniature pick-axe to escape from the egg.
   IV. The offspring of all higher-order animals originate from single egg cells that are carried by mothers, and most of these eggs are relatively small, often microscopic.
   V. The egg of the African ostrich, however, weighs a massive thirty pounds, making it the largest single cell on earth, and a common object of human curiosity and wonder.

   The BEST order is:
   A. V, IV, I, II, III   B. I, IV, V, III, II   C. IV, II, III, V, I   D. IV, V, II, III, I

   1.____

2.
   I. Typically only a few feet high on the open sea, individual tsunami have been known to circle the entire globe two or three times if their progress is not interrupted, but are not usually dangerous until they approach the shallow water that surrounds land masses.
   II. Some of the most terrifying and damaging hazards caused by earthquakes are tsunami, which were once called "tidal waves"—a poorly chosen name, since these waves have nothing to do with tides.
   III. Then a wave, slowed by the sudden drag on the lower part of its moving water column, will pile upon itself, sometimes reaching a height of over 100 feet.
   IV. Tsunami (Japanese for "great harbor wave") are seismic waves that are caused by earthquakes near oceanic trenches, and once triggered, can travel up to 600 miles an hour on the open ocean.
   V. A land-shoaling tsunami is capable of extraordinary destruction; some tsunami have deposited large boats miles inland, washed out two-foot-thick seawalls, and scattered locomotive trains over long distances.

   The BEST order is:
   A. IV, I, III, II, V   B. I, III, IV, II, V   C. V, I, III, II, IV   D. II, IV, I, III, V

   2.____

3.
   I. Soon, by the 1940s, jazz was the most popular type of music among American intellectuals and college students.
   II. In the early days of jazz, it was considered "lowdown" music, or music that was played only in rough, disreputable bars and taverns.
   III. However, jazz didn't take too long to develop from early ragtime melodies into more complex, sophisticated forms, such as Charlie Parker's "bebop" style of jazz.
   IV. After charismatic band leaders such as Duke Ellington and Count Basie brought jazz to a larger audience, and jazz continued to evolve into more complicated forms, white audiences began to accept and even to enjoy the new American art form.
   V. Many white Americans, who then dictated the tastes of society, were wary of music that was played almost exclusively in black clubs in the poorer sections of cities and towns.

   The BEST order is:
   A. V, IV, III, II, I   B. II, V, III, IV, I   C. IV, V, III, I, II   D. I, II, IV, III, V

   3._____

4.
   I. Then, hanging in a windless place, the magnetized end of the needle would always point to the south.
   II. The needle could then be balanced on the rim of a cup, or the edge of a fingernail, but this balancing act was hard to maintain, and the needle often fell off.
   III. Other needles would point to the north, and it was important for any traveler finding his way with a compass to remember which kind of magnetized needle he was carrying.
   IV. To make some of the earliest compasses in recorded history, ancient Chinese "magicians" would rub a needle with a piece of magnetized iron called a lodestone.
   V. A more effective method of keeping the needle free to swing with its magnetic pull was to attach a strand of silk to the center of the needle with a tiny piece of wax.

   The BEST order is:
   A. IV, II, V, I, III   B. IV, III, V, II, I   C. IV, V, II, I, III   D. IV, I, III, V, II

   4._____

5.
   I The now-famous first mate of the *H.M.S. Bounty*, Fletcher Christian, founded one of the world's most peculiar civilizations in 1790.
   II. The men knew they had just committed a crime for which they could be hanged, so they set sail for Pitcairn, a remote, abandoned island in the far eastern region of the Polynesian archipelago, accompanied by twelve Polynesian women and six men.
   III. In a mutiny that has become legendary, Christian and the others forced Captain Bligh into a lifeboat and set him adrift off the coast of Tonga in April of 1789.
   IV. In early 1790, the *Bounty* landed at Pitcairn Island, where the men lived out the rest of their lives and founded an isolated community which to this day includes direct descendants of Christian and the other Crewmen.

   5._____

V. The *Bounty*, commanded by Captain William Bligh, was in the middle of a global voyage, and Christian and his shipmates had come to the conclusion that Bligh was a reckless madman who would lead them to their deaths unless they took the ship from him.

The BEST order is:
A. IV, V, III, II, I   B. I, III, V, II, IV   C. I, V, III, II, IV   D. III, I, V, IV, II

6. I. But once the vines had been led to make orchids, the flowers had to be carefully hand-pollinated, because unpollinated orchids usually lasted less than a day, wilting and dropping off the vine before it had even become dark.
    II. The Totonac farmers discovered that looping a vine back around once it reached a five-foot height on its host tree would cause the vine to flower.
    III. Though they knew how to process the fruit pods and extract vanilla's flavoring agent, the Totonacs also knew that a wild vanilla vine did not produce abundant flowers or fruit.
    IV. Wild vines climbed along the trunks and canopies of trees, and this constant upward growth diverted most of the vine's energy to making leaves instead of the orchid flowers that once pollinated, would produce the flavorful pods.
    V. Hundreds of years before vanilla became a prized food flavoring in Europe and the Western World, the Totonac Indians of the Mexican Gulf Coast were skilled cultivators of the vanilla vine, whose fruit they literally worshipped as a goddess.

    The BEST order is:
    A. II, III, IV, I, V   B. II, IV, III, I, V   C. V, III, IV, II, I   D. III, IV, I, II, V

7. I. Once airborne, the spider is at the mercy of the air currents—usually the spider takes a brief journey, traveling close to the ground, but some have been found in air samples collected as high as 10,000 feet, or been reported landing on ships far out at sea.
    II. Once a young spider has hatched, it must leave the environment into which it was born as quickly as possible, in order to avoid competing with its hundreds of brothers and sisters for food.
    III. The silk rises into warm air currents, and as soon as the pull feels adequate the spider lets go and drifts up into the air, suspended from the silk strand in the same way that a person might parasail.
    IV. To help young spiders do this, many species have adapted a practice known as "aerial dispersal," or, in common speech, "ballooning."
    V. A spider that wants to leave its surroundings quickly will climb to the top of a grass system or twig, face into the wind, and aim its back end into the air, releasing a long stream of silk from the glands near the tip of its abdomen.

    The BEST order is:
    A. V, IV, II, III, I   B. V, II, IV, I, III   C. II, V, IV, III, I   D. II, IV, V, III, I

8. I. For about a year, Tycho worked at a castle in Prague with a scientist named Johannes Kepler, but their association was cut short by another argument that drove Kepler out of the castle, to later develop, on his own, the theory of planetary orbits.
    II. Tycho found life without a nose embarrassing, so he made a new nose for himself out of silver, which reportedly remained glued to his face for the rest of his life.
    III. Tycho Brahe, the 17th-century Danish astronomer, is today more famous for his odd and arrogant personality than for any contribution he has made to our knowledge of the stars and planets.
    IV. Early in his career, as a student at Rostock University, Tycho got into an argument with another student about who was the better mathematician, and the two became so angry that the argument turned into a sword fight, during which Tycho's nose was sliced off.
    V. Later in his life, Tycho's arrogance may have kept him from playing a part in one of the greatest astronomical discoveries in history: the elliptical orbits of the solar system's planets.
    The BEST order is:
    A. I, IV, II, III, V   B. IV, II, III, V, I   C. IV, II, I, III, V   D. III, IV, II, V, I

9. I. The processionaries are so used to this routine that if a person picks up the end of a silk line and brings it back to the origin—creating a closed circle—the caterpillars may travel around and around for days, sometimes starving or freezing, without changing course.
    II. Rather than relying on sight or sound, the other caterpillars, who are lined up end-to-end behind the leader, travel to and from their nests by walking on this silk line, and each will reinforce it by laying down its own marking line as it passes over.
    III. In order to insure the safety of individuals, the processionary caterpillar nests in a tree with dozens of other caterpillars, and at night, when it is safest, they all leave together in search of food.
    IV. The processionary caterpillar of the European continent is a perfect illustration of how much some inspect species rely on instinct in their daily routines.
    V. As they leave their nests, the processionaries form a single-file line behind a leader who spins and lays out a silk line to mark the chosen path.
    The BEST order is:
    A. IV, III, V, II, I   B. III, V, IV, II, I   C. III, V, II, I, IV   D. IV, V, III, I, II

10. I. Often, the child is also given a handcrafted walker or push cart, to provide support for its first upright explorations.
    II. In traditional Indian families, a child's first steps are celebrated as a ceremonial event, rooted in ancient myth.
    III. These carts are often intricately designed to resemble the chariot of Krishna, an important figure in Indian mythology.
    IV. The sound of these anklet bells is intended to mimic the footsteps of the legendary child Rama, who is celebrated in devotional songs throughout India.

V. When the child's parents see that the child is ready to begin walking, they will fit it with specially designed ankle bracelets, adorned with gently ringing bells.

The BEST order is:
A. II, III, IV, I, V B. II, V, III, I, IV C. V, IV, I, III, II D. V, III, II, I, IV

11. I. The settlers planted Osage oranges all across Middle America, and today long lines and rectangles of Osage orange trees can still be seen on the prairies, running along the former boundaries of farms that no longer exist.
II. After trying sod walls and water-filled ditches with no success, American farmers began to look for a plant that was adaptable to prairie weather, and that could be trimmed into a hedge that was "pig-tight, horse-high, and bull-strong."
III. The tree, so named because it bore a large (but inedible) fruit the size of an orange, was among the sturdiest and hardiest of American trees, and was prized among Native Americans for the strength and flexibility of bows which were made from its wood.
IV. The first people to practice agriculture on the American flatlands were faced with an important problem: what would they use to fence their land in a place that was almost entirely without trees or rocks?
V. Finally, an Illinois farmer brought the settlers a tree that was native to the land between the Red and Arkansas rivers, a tree called the Osage orange.

The BEST order is:
A. II, I, V, III, IV B. I, II, III, IV, V C. IV, II, V, III, I D. IV, II, I, III, V

11.____

12. I. After about ten minutes of such spirited and complicated activity, the head dancer is free to make up his or her own movements while maintaining the interest of the New Year's crowd.
II. The dancer will then perform a series of leg kicks, while at the same time operating the lion's mouth with his own hand and moving the ears and eyes by means of a string which is attached to the dancer's own mouth.
III. The most difficult role of this dance belongs to the one who controls the lion's head; this person must lead all the other "parts" of the lion through the choreographed segments of the dance.
IV. The head dancer begins with a complex series of steps. alternately stepping forward with the head raised, and then retreating a few steps while lowering the head, a movement that is intended to create the impression that the lion is keeping a watchful eye for anything evil.
V. When performing a traditional Chinese New Year's lion dance, several performers must fit themselves inside a large lion costume and work together to enact different parts of the dance.

The BEST order is:
A. V, III, IV, II, I B. III, IV, II, V, I C. III, I, V, IV, II D. IV, II, III, V, I

12.____

13. I. For many years the shell of the chambered nautilus was treasured in Europe for its beauty and intricacy, but collectors were unaware that they were in possession of the structure that marked a "missing link" in the evolution of marine mollusks.
    II. The nautilus, however, evolved a series of enclosed chambers in its shell, and invented a new use for the structure: the shell began to serve as a buoyancy device.
    III. Equipped with this new flotation device, the nautilus did not need the single, muscular foot of its predecessors, but instead developed flaps, tentacles, and a gentle form of jet propulsion that transformed it into the first mollusk able to take command of its own density and explore a three-dimensional world.
    IV. By pumping and adjusting air pressure into the chambers, the nautilus could spend the day resting on the bottom, and then rise toward the surface at night in search of food.
    V. The nautilus shell looks like a large snail shell, similar to those of its ancestors, who used their shells as protective coverings while they were anchored to the sea floor.
    The BEST order is:
    A. V, II, IV, I, III   B. V, I, II, III, IV   C. I, II, V, III, IV   D. I, V, II, IV, III

14. I. While France and England battled for control of the region, the Acadiens prospered on the fertile farmland, which was finally secured by England in 1713.
    II. Early in the 17th century, settlers from Western France founded a colony called Acadie in what is now the Canadian province of Nova Scotia.
    III. At this time, English officials feared the presence of spies among the Acadiens who might be loyal to their French homeland, and the Acadiens were deported to spots along the Atlantic and Caribbean shores of America.
    IV. The French settlers remained on this land, under English rule, for around forty years, until the beginning of the French and Indian War, another conflict between France and England.
    V. As the Acadien refugees drifted toward a final home in Southern Louisiana, neighbors shortened their name to "Cadien," and finally "Cajun," the name which the descendants of early Acadiens still call themselves.
    The BEST order is:
    A. I, IV, II, III, V   B. II, I, III, V, IV   C. II, I, IV, III, V   D. V, II, III, IV, I

15. I. Traditional households in the Eastern and Western regions of Africa serve two meals a day—one at around noon, and the other in the evening.
    II. The starch is then used in the way that Americans might use a spoon, to scoop up a portion of the main dish on the person's plate.
    III. The reason for the starch's inclusion in every meal has to do with taste as well as nutrition; African food can be very spicy, and the starch is known to cool the burning effect of the main dish.
    IV. When serving these meals, the main dish is usually served on individual plates, and the starch is served on a communal plate, from which diners break off a piece of bread or scoop rice or fufu in their fingers.

V. The typical meals usually consist of a thick stew or soup as the main course, and an accompanying starch—either bread, rice, or *fufu*, a starchy grain paste similar in consistency to mashed potatoes.

The BEST order is:

A. V, II, III, IV, I   B. V, I, IV, III, II   C. I, IV, V, III, II   D. I, V, IV, II, III

16.
  I. In the early days of the American Midwest, Indiana settlers sometimes came together to hold an event called an apple peeling, where neighboring settlers gathered at the homestead of a host family to help prepare the hosts' apple crop for cooking, canning, and making apple butter.
  II. At the beginning of the event, each peeler sat down in front of a ten- or twenty-gallon stone jar and was given a crock of apples and a paring knife.
  III. Once a peeler had finished with a crock, another was placed next to him; if the peeler was an unmarried man, he kept a strict count of the number of apples he had peeled, because the winner was allowed to kiss the girl of his choice.
  IV. The peeling usually ended by 9:30 in the evening, when the neighbors gathered in the host family's parlor for a dance social.
  V. The apples were peeled, cored, and quartered, and then placed into the jar.

  The BEST order is:

  A. I, V, III, IV, II   B. II, V, III, IV, I   C. I, II, V, III, IV   D. II, I, V, IV, III

16.____

17.
  I. If your pet turtle is a land turtle and is native to temperate climates, it will stop eating some time in October, which should be your cue to prepare the turtle for hibernation.
  II. The box should then be covered with a wire screen, which will protect the turtle from any rodents or predators that might want to take advantage of a motionless and helpless animal.
  III. When your turtle hasn't eaten for a while and appears ready to hibernate, it should be moved to its winter quarters, most likely a cellar or garage, where the temperature should range between 40° and 45°F.
  IV. Instead of feeding the turtle, you should bathe it every day in warm water, to encourage the turtle to empty its intestines in preparation for its long winter sleep.
  V. Here the turtle should be placed in a well-ventilated box whose bottom is covered with a moisture-absorbing layer of clay beads, and then filled three-fourths full with almost dry peat moss or wood chips, into which the turtle will burrow and sleep for several months.

  The BEST order is:

  A. I, IV, III, V, II   B. III, IV, II, V, I   C. III, II, IV, I, V   D. IV, V, II, III, I

17.____

18.
  I. Once he has reached the nest, the hunter uses two sturdy bamboo poles like huge chopsticks to pull the next away from the mountainside, into a large basket that will be lowered to people waiting below.
  II. The world's largest honeybees colonize the Nealese mountainsides, building honeycombs as large as a person on sheer rock faces that are often hundreds of feet high.

18.____

III. In the remote mountain country of Nepal, a small band of "honey hunters" carry out a tradition so ancient that 10,000 year-old drawings of the practice have been found in the caves of Nepal.
IV. To harvest the honey and beeswax from these combs, a honey hunter climbs above the nests, lowers a long bamboo-fiber ladder over the cliff, and then climbs down.
V. Throughout this dangerous practice, the hunter is stung repeatedly, and only the veterans, with skin that has been toughened over the years, are able to return from a hunt without the painful swelling caused by stings.

The BEST order is:
A. II, IV, III, V, I   B. II, IV, I, V, III   C. V, III, II, IV, I   D. III, II, IV, I, V

19. I. After the Romans left Britain, there were relentless attacks on the islands from the barbarian tribes of northern Germany—the Angles, Saxons, and Jutes.
    II. As the empire weakened, Roman soldiers withdrew from Britain, leaving behind a country that continued to practice the Christian religion that had been introduced by the Romans.
    III. Early Latin writings tell of a Christian warrior named Arturius (Arthur, in English) who led the British citizens to defeat these barbarian invades, and brought an extended period of peace to the lands of Britain.
    IV. Long ago, the British Isles were part of the far-flung Roman Empire that extended across most of Europe and into Africa and Asia.
    V. The romantic legend of King Arthur and his knights of the Round Table, one of the most popular and widespread stories of all time, appears to have some foundation in history.

    The BEST order is:
    A. V, IV, III, II, I   B. V, IV, II, I, III   C. IV, V, II, III, I   D. IV, III, II, I, V

20. I. The cylinder was allowed to cool until it could stand on its own, and then it was cut from the tube and split down the side with a single straight cut.
    II. Nineteenth-century glassmakers, who had not yet discovered the glazier's modern techniques for making panes of glass, had to create a method for converting their blown gas into flat sheets.
    III. The bubble was then pierced at the end to make a hole that opened up while the glassmaker gently spun it, creating a cylinder of glass.
    IV. Turned on its side and laid on a conveyor belt, the cylinder was strengthened, or tempered, by being heated again and cooled very slowly, eventually flattening out into a single rectangular of glass.
    V. To do this, the glassmaker dipped the end of a long tube into melted glass and blew into the other end of the tube, creating an expanding bubble of glass.

    The BEST order is:
    A. II, V, III, IV, I   B. II, IV, V, III, I   C. III, V, II, IV, I   D. III, I, IV, V, II

21. I. The splints are almost always hidden, but horses are occasionally born whose splinted toes project from the leg on either side, just above the hoof.
    II. The second and fourth toes remained, but shrank to thin splints of bone that fused invisibly to the horse's leg bone.
    III. Horses are unique among mammals, having evolved feet that each end in what is essentially a single toe, capped by a large, sturdy hoof.
    IV. Julius Caesar, an emperor of ancient Rome, was said to have owned one of these three-toed horses, and considered it so special that he would not permit anyone else to ride it.
    V. Though the horse's earlier ancestors possessed the traditional mammalian set of five toes on each foot, the horse has retained only its third toe; its first and fifth toes disappeared completely as the horse evolved.

    The BEST order is:
    A. III, V, II, I, IV   B. V, III, II, IV, I   C. III, II, V, I, IV   D. V, II, III, I, IV

22. I. The new building materials—some of which are twenty feet long, and weigh nearly six tons—were transported to Pohnpei on rafts, and were brought into their present position by using hibiscus fiber ropes and leverage to move the stone columns upward along the inclined trunks of coconut palm trees.
    II. The ancestors built great fires to heat the stone, and then poured cool seawater on the columns, which caused the stone to contract and split along natural fracture lines.
    III. The now-abandoned enclave of Nan Madol, a group of 92 man-made islands off the shore of the Micronesian island of Pohnpei, is estimated to have been built around the year 500 A.D.
    IV. The islanders say their ancestors quarried stone columns from a nearby island, where large basalt columns were formed by the cooling of molten lava.
    V. The structures of Nan Madol are remarkable for the sheer size of some of the stone "longs" or columns that were used to create the walls of the offshore community, and today anthropologists can only rely on the information of existing local people for clues about how Nan Madol was built.

    The BEST order is:
    A. V, IV, III, II, I   B. V, III, I, IV, II   C. III, V, IV, II, I   D. III, I, IV, II, V

23. I. One of the most easily manipulated substances on earth, glass can be made into ceramic tiles that are composed of over 90% air.
    II. NASA's space shuttles are the first spacecraft ever designed to leave and re-enter the earth's atmosphere while remaining intact.
    III. These ceramic tiles are such effective insulators that when a tile emerges from the oven in which it was fired, it can be held safely in a person's hand by the edges while its interior still glows at a temperature well over 2000°F.
    IV. Eventually, the engineers were led to a material that is as old as our most ancient civilization.
    V. Because the temperature during atmospheric re-entry is so incredibly hot, it took NASA's engineers some time to find a substance capable of protecting the shuttles.

The BEST order is:
A. V, II, I, II, IV   B. II, V, IV, I, III   C. II, III, I, IV, V   D. V, IV, III, I, II

24. I. The secret to teaching any parakeet to talk is patience, and the understanding that when a bird talks," it is simply imitating what it hears, rather than putting ideas into words.
 II. You should stay just out of sight of the bird and repeat the phrase you want it to learn, for at least fifteen minutes every morning and evening.
 III. It is important to leave the bird without any words of encouragement or farewell; otherwise it might combine stray remarks or phrases, such as "Good night," with the phrase you are trying to teach it.
 IV. For this reason, to train your bird to imitate your words you should keep it free of any distractions, especially other noises, while you are giving it "lesson."
 V. After your repetition, you should quietly leave the bird alone for a while, to think over what it has just heard.
The BEST order is:
A. I, IV, II, V, III   B. I, II, IV, III, V   C. III, II, I, V, IV   D. III, I, V, IV, II

25. I. As a school approaches, fishermen from neighboring communities join their fishing boats together as a fleet, and string their gill nets together to make a huge fence that is held up by cork floats.
 II. At a signal from the party leaders, or *nakura*, the family members pound the sides of the boats or beat the water with long poles, creating a sudden and deafening noise.
 III. The fishermen work together to drag the trap into a half-circle that may reach 300 yards in diameter, and then the families move their boats to form the other half of the circle around the school of fish.
 IV. The school of fish flee from the commotion into the awaiting trap, where a final wall of net is thrown over the open end of the half-circle, securing the day's haul.
 V. Indonesian people from the area around the Sulu islands live on the sea, in floating villages made of lashed-together or stilted homes, and make much of their living by fishing their home waters for migrating schools of snapper, scad, and other fish.
The BEST order is:
A. I, V, III, IV, II   B. I, II, IV, III, V   C. V, I, II, III, IV   D. V, I, III, II, IV

KEY (CORRECT ANSWERS)

1.	D	11.	C
2.	D	12.	A
3.	B	13.	D
4.	A	14.	C
5.	C	15.	D
6.	C	16.	C
7.	D	17.	A
8.	D	18.	D
9.	A	19.	B
10.	B	20.	A

21.	A
22.	C
23.	B
24.	A
25.	D

PHILOSOPHY, PRINCIPLES, PRACTICES, AND TECHNICS OF SUPERVISION, ADMINISTRATION, MANAGEMENT, AND ORGANIZATION

TABLE OF CONTENTS

	Page
MEANING OF SUPERVISION	1
THE OLD AND THE NEW SUPERVISION	1
THE EIGHT (8) BASIC PRINCIPLES OF THE NEW SUPERVISION	1
I. Principle of Responsibility	1
II. Principle of Authority	2
III. Principle of Self-Growth	2
IV. Principle of Individual Worth	2
V. Principle of Creative Leadership	2
VI. Principle of Success and Failure	2
VII. Principle of Science	3
VIII. Principle of Cooperation	3
WHAT IS ADMINISTRATION?	3
I. Practices Commonly Classed as "Supervisory"	3
II. Practices Commonly Classed as "Administrative"	3
III. Practices Commonly Classed as Both "Supervisory" and "Administrative"	4
RESPONSIBILITIES OF THE SUPERVISOR	4
COMPETENCIES OF THE SUPERVISOR	4
THE PROFESSIONAL SUPERVISOR-EMPLOYEE RELATIONSHIP	4
MINI-TEXT IN SUPERVISION, ADMINISTRATION, MANAGEMENT, AND ORGANIZATION	5
I. Brief Highlights	5
A. Levels of Management	6
B. What the Supervisor Must Learn	6
C. A Definition of Supervision	6
D. Elements of the Team Concept	6
E. Principles of Organization	6
F. The Four Important Parts of Every Job	7
G. Principles of Delegation	7
H. Principles of Effective Communications	7
I. Principles of Work Improvement	7
J. Areas of Job Improvement	7
K. Seven Key Points in Making Improvements	8

	L.	Corrective Techniques for Job Improvement	8
	M.	A Planning Checklist	8
	N.	Five Characteristics of Good Directions	9
	O.	Types of Directions	9
	P.	Controls	9
	Q.	Orienting the New Employee	9
	R.	Checklist for Orienting New Employees	9
	S.	Principles of Learning	10
	T.	Causes of Poor Performance	10
	U.	Four Major Steps in On-the-Job Instructions	10
	V.	Employees Want Five Things	10
	W.	Some Don'ts in Regard to Praise	11
	X.	How to Gain Your Workers' Confidence	11
	Y.	Sources of Employee Problems	11
	Z.	The Supervisor's Key to Discipline	11
	AA.	Five Important Processes of Management	12
	BB.	When the Supervisor Fails to Plan	12
	CC.	Fourteen General Principles of Management	12
	DD.	Change	12
II.	Brief Topical Summaries		13
	A.	Who/What is the Supervisor?	13
	B.	The Sociology of Work	13
	C.	Principles and Practices of Supervision	14
	D.	Dynamic Leadership	14
	E.	Processes for Solving Problems	15
	F.	Training for Results	15
	G.	Health, Safety, and Accident Prevention	16
	H.	Equal Employment Opportunity	16
	I.	Improving Communications	16
	J.	Self-Development	17
	K.	Teaching and Training	17
		1. The Teaching Process	17
		a. Preparation	17
		b. Presentation	18
		c. Summary	18
		d. Application	18
		e. Evaluation	18
		2. Teaching Methods	18
		a. Lecture	18
		b. Discussion	18
		c. Demonstration	19
		d. Performance	19
		e. Which Method to Use	19

PHILOSOPHY, PRINCIPLES, PRACTICES, AND TECHNICS
OF
SUPERVISION, ADMINISTRATION, MANAGEMENT, AND ORGANIZATION

MEANING OF SUPERVISION

The extension of the democratic philosophy has been accompanied by an extension in the scope of supervision. Modern leaders and supervisors no longer think of supervision in the narrow sense of being confined chiefly to visiting employees, supplying materials, or rating the staff. They regard supervision as being intimately related to all the concerned agencies of society, they speak of the supervisor's function in terms of "growth," rather than the "improvement" of employees.

This modern concept of supervision may be defined as follows: Supervision is leadership and the development of leadership within groups which are cooperatively engaged in inspection, research, training, guidance, and evaluation.

THE OLD AND THE NEW SUPERVISION

TRADITIONAL
1. Inspection
2. Focused on the employee
3. Visitation
4. Random and haphazard
5. Imposed and authoritarian
6. One person usually

MODERN
1. Study and analysis
2. Focused on aims, materials, methods, supervisors, employees, environment
3. Demonstrations, intervisitation, workshops, directed reading, bulletins, etc.
4. Definitely organized and planned (scientific)
5. Cooperative and democratic
6. Many persons involved (creative)

THE EIGHT (8) BASIC PRINCIPLES OF THE NEW SUPERVISION

I. Principle of Responsibility
   Authority to act and responsibility for acting must be joined.
   A. If you give responsibility, give authority.
   B. Define employee duties clearly.
   C. Protect employees from criticism by others.
   D. Recognize the rights as well as obligations of employees.
   E. Achieve the aims of a democratic society insofar as it is possible within the area of your work.
   F. Establish a situation favorable to training and learning.
   G. Accept ultimate responsibility for everything done in your section, unit, office, division, department.
   H. Good administration and good supervision are inseparable.

II. Principle of Authority
The success of the supervisor is measured by the extent to which the power of authority is not used.
   A. Exercise simplicity and informality in supervision
   B. Use the simplest machinery of supervision
   C. If it is good for the organization as a whole, it is probably justified.
   D. Seldom be arbitrary or authoritative.
   E. Do not base your work on the power of position or of personality.
   F. Permit and encourage the free expression of opinions.

III. Principle of Self-Growth
The success of the supervisor is measured by the extent to which, and the speed with which, he is no longer needed.
   A. Base criticism on principles, not on specifics.
   B. Point out higher activities to employees.
   C. Train for self-thinking by employees to meet new situations.
   D. Stimulate initiative, self-reliance, and individual responsibility
   E. Concentrate on stimulating the growth of employees rather than on removing defects.

IV. Principle of Individual Worth
Respect for the individual is a paramount consideration in supervision.
   A. Be human and sympathetic in dealing with employees.
   B. Don't nag about things to be done.
   C. Recognize the individual differences among employees and seek opportunities to permit best expression of each personality.

V. Principle of Creative Leadership
The best supervision is that which is not apparent to the employee.
   A. Stimulate, don't drive employees to creative action.
   B. Emphasize doing good things.
   C. Encourage employees to do what they do best.
   D. Do not be too greatly concerned with details of subject or method.
   E. Do not be concerned exclusively with immediate problems and activities.
   F. Reveal higher activities and make them both desired and maximally possible.
   G. Determine procedures in the light of each situation but see that these are derived from a sound basic philosophy.
   H. Aid, inspire, and lead so as to liberate the creative spirit latent in all good employees.

VI. Principle of Success and Failure
There are no unsuccessful employees, only unsuccessful supervisors who have failed to give proper leadership.
   A. Adapt suggestions to the capacities, attitudes, and prejudices of employees.
   B. Be gradual, be progressive, be persistent.
   C. Help the employee find the general principle; have the employee apply his own problem to the general principle.
   D. Give adequate appreciation for good work and honest effort.
   E. Anticipate employee difficulties and help to prevent them.
   F. Encourage employees to do the desirable things they will do anyway.
   G. Judge your supervision by the results it secures.

VII. Principle of Science
Successful supervision is scientific, objective, and experimental. It is based on facts, not on prejudices.
  A. Be cumulative in results.
  B. Never divorce your suggestions from the goals of training.
  C. Don't be impatient of results.
  D. Keep all matters on a professional, not a personal, level.
  E. Do not be concerned exclusively with immediate problems and activities.
  F. Use objective means of determining achievement and rating where possible.

VIII. Principle of Cooperation
Supervision is a cooperative enterprise between supervisor and employee.
  A. Begin with conditions as they are.
  B. Ask opinions of all involved when formulating policies.
  C. Organization is as good as its weakest link.
  D. Let employees help to determine policies and department programs.
  E. Be approachable and accessible—physically and mentally.
  F. Develop pleasant social relationships.

WHAT IS ADMINISTRATION

Administration is concerned with providing the environment, the material facilities, and the operational procedures that will promote the maximum growth and development of supervisors and employees. (Organization is an aspect and a concomitant of administration.)

There is no sharp line of demarcation between supervision and administration; these functions are intimately interrelated and, often, overlapping. They are complementary activities.

I. Practices Commonly Classed as "Supervisory"
  A. Conducting employees' conferences
  B. Visiting sections, units, offices, divisions, departments
  C. Arranging for demonstrations
  D. Examining plans
  E. Suggesting professional reading
  F. Interpreting bulletins
  G. Recommending in-service training courses
  H. Encouraging experimentation
  I. Appraising employee morale
  J. Providing for intervisitation

II. Practices Commonly Classified as "Administrative"
  A. Management of the office
  B. Arrangement of schedules for extra duties
  C. Assignment of rooms or areas
  D. Distribution of supplies
  E. Keeping records and reports
  F. Care of audio-visual materials
  G. Keeping inventory records
  H. Checking record cards and books

I. Programming special activities
   J. Checking on the attendance and punctuality of employees

III. Practices Commonly Classified as Both "Supervisory" and "Administrative"
   A. Program construction
   B. Testing or evaluating outcomes
   C. Personnel accounting
   D. Ordering instructional materials

RESPONSIBILITIES OF THE SUPERVISOR

A person employed in a supervisory capacity must constantly be able to improve his own efficiency and ability. He represent the employer to the employees and only continuous self-examination can make him a capable supervisor.

Leadership and training are the supervisor's responsibility. An efficient working unit is one in which the employees work with the supervisor. It is his job to bring out the best in his employees. He must always be relaxed, courteous, and calm in his association with his employees. Their feelings are important, and a harsh attitude does not develop the most efficient employees.

COMPETENCES OF THE SUPERVISOR

   I. Complete knowledge of the duties and responsibilities of his position.
   II. To be able to organize a job, plan ahead, and carry through.
   III. To have self-confidence and initiative.
   IV. To be able to handle the unexpected situation and make quick decisions.
   V. To be able to properly train subordinates in the positions they are best suited for.
   VI. To be able to keep good human relations among his subordinates.
   VII. To be able to keep good human relations between his subordinates and himself and to earn their respect and trust.

THE PROFESSIONAL SUPERVISOR-EMPLOYEE RELATIONSHIP

There are two kinds of efficiency: one kind is only apparent and is produced in organizations through the exercise of mere discipline; this is but a simulation of the second, or true, efficiency which springs from spontaneous cooperation. If you are a manager, no matter how great or small your responsibility, it is your job, in the final analysis, to create and develop this involuntary cooperation among the people whom you supervise. For, no matter how powerful a combination of money, machines, and materials a company may have, this is a dead and sterile thing without a team of willing, thinking, and articulate people to guide it.

The following 21 points are presented as indicative of the exemplary basic relationship that should exist between supervisor and employee:

1. Each person wants to be liked and respected by his fellow employee and wants to be treated with consideration and respect by his superior.
2. The most competent employee will make an error. However, in a unit where good relations exist between the supervisor and his employees, tenseness and fear do not exist. Thus, errors are not hidden or covered up, and the efficiency of a unit is not impaired.

3. Subordinates resent rules, regulations, or orders that are unreasonable or unexplained.
4. Subordinates are quick to resent unfairness, harshness, injustices, and favoritism.
5. An employee will accept responsibility if he knows that he will be complimented for a job well done, and not too harshly chastised for failure; that his supervisor will check the cause of the failure, and, if it was the supervisor's fault, he will assume the blame therefore. If it was the employee's fault, his supervisor will explain the correct method or means of handling the responsibility.
6. An employee wants to receive credit for a suggestion he has made, that is used. If a suggestion cannot be used, the employee is entitled to an explanation. The supervisor should not say "no" and close the subject.
7. Fear and worry slow up a worker's ability. Poor working environment can impair his physical and mental health. A good supervisor avoids forceful methods, threats, and arguments to get a job done.
8. A forceful supervisor is able to train his employees individually and as a team, and is able to motivate them in the proper channels.
9. A mature supervisor is able to properly evaluate his subordinates and to keep them happy and satisfied.
10. A sensitive supervisor will never patronize his subordinates.
11. A worthy supervisor will respect his employees' confidences.
12. Definite and clear-cut responsibilities should be assigned to each executive.
13. Responsibility should always be coupled with corresponding authority.
14. No change should be made in the scope or responsibilities of a position without a definite understanding to that effect on the part of all persons concerned.
15. No executive or employee, occupying a single position in the organization, should be subject to definite orders from more than one source.
16. Orders should never be given to subordinates over the head of a responsible executive. Rather than do this, the officer in question should be supplanted.
17. Criticisms of subordinates should, whoever possible, be made privately, and in no case should a subordinate be criticized in the presence of executives or employees of equal or lower rank.
18. No dispute or difference between executives or employees as to authority or responsibilities should be considered too trivial for prompt and careful adjudication.
19. Promotions, wage changes, and disciplinary action should always be approved by the executive immediately superior to the one directly responsible.
20. No executive or employee should ever be required, or expected, to be at the same time an assistant to, and critic of, another.
21. Any executive whose work is subject to regular inspection should, wherever practicable, be given the assistance and facilities necessary to enable him to maintain an independent check of the quality of his work.

MINI-TEXT IN SUPERVISION, ADMINISTRATION, MANAGEMENT, AND ORGANIZATION

I. Brief Highlights

Listed concisely and sequentially are major headings and important data in the field for quick recall and review.

A. Levels of Management
Any organization of some size has several levels of management. In terms of a ladder, the levels are:

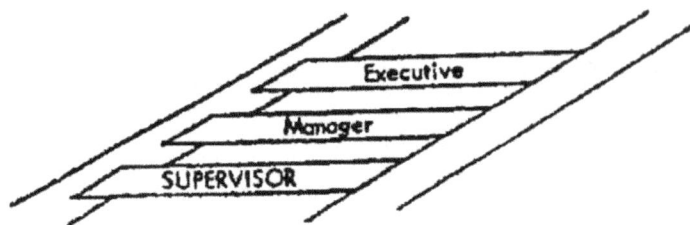

The first level is very important because it is the beginning point of management leadership.

B. What the Supervisor Must Learn
A supervisor must learn to:
1. Deal with people and their differences
2. Get the job done through people
3. Recognize the problems when they exist
4. Overcome obstacles to good performance
5. Evaluate the performance of people
6. Check his own performance in terms of accomplishment

C. A Definition of Supervisor
The term supervisor means any individual having authority, in the interests of the employer, to hire, transfer, suspend, lay-off, recall, promote, discharge, assign, reward, or discipline other employees or responsibility to direct them, or to adjust their grievances, or effectively to recommend such action, if, in connection with the foregoing, exercise of such authority is not of a merely routine or clerical nature but requires the use of independent judgment.

D. Elements of the Team Concept
What is involved in teamwork? The component parts are:
1. Members
2. A leader
3. Goals
4. Plans
5. Cooperation
6. Spirit

E. Principles of Organization
1. A team member must know what his job is.
2. Be sure that the nature and scope of a job are understood.
3. Authority and responsibility should be carefully spelled out.
4. A supervisor should be permitted to make the maximum number of decisions affecting his employees.
5. Employees should report to only one supervisor.
6. A supervisor should direct only as many employees as he can handle effectively.
7. An organization plan should be flexible.

8. Inspection and performance of work should be separate.
9. Organizational problems should receive immediate attention.
10. Assign work in line with ability and experience.

F. The Four Important Parts of Every Job
1. Inherent in every job is the *accountability* for results.
2. A second set of factors in every job is *responsibilities*.
3. Along with duties and responsibilities one must have the *authority* to act within certain limits without obtaining permission to proceed.
4. No job exists in a vacuum. The supervisor is surrounded by key *relationships*.

G. Principles of Delegation
Where work is delegated for the first time, the supervisor should think in terms of these questions:
1. Who is best qualified to do this?
2. Can an employee improve his abilities by doing this?
3. How long should an employee spend on this?
4. Are there any special problems for which he will need guidance?
5. How broad a delegation can I make?

H. Principles of Effective Communications
1. Determine the media.
2. To whom directed?
3. Identification and source authority.
4. Is communication understood?

I. Principles of Work Improvement
1. Most people usually do only the work which is assigned to them.
2. Workers are likely to fit assigned work into the time available to perform it.
3. A good workload usually stimulates output.
4. People usually do their best work when they know that results will be reviewed or inspected.
5. Employees usually feel that someone else is responsible for conditions of work, workplace layout, job methods, type of tools/equipment, and other such factors.
6. Employees are usually defensive about their job security.
7. Employees have natural resistance to change.
8. Employees can support or destroy a supervisor.
9. A supervisor usually earns the respect of his people through his personal example of diligence and efficiency.

J. Areas of Job Improvement
The areas of job improvement are quite numerous, but the most common ones which a supervisor can identify and utilize are:
1. Departmental layout
2. Flow of work
3. Workplace layout
4. Utilization of manpower
5. Work methods
6. Materials handling

7. Utilization
8. Motion economy

K. Seven Key Points in Making Improvements
1. Select the job to be improved
2. Study how it is being done now
3. Question the present method
4. Determine actions to be taken
5. Chart proposed method
6. Get approval and apply
7. Solicit worker participation

l. Corrective Techniques of Job Improvement
Specific Problems
1. Size of workload
2. Inability to meet schedules
3. Strain and fatigue
4. Improper use of men and skills
5. Waste, poor quality, unsafe conditions
6. Bottleneck conditions that hinder output
7. Poor utilization of equipment and machine
8. Efficiency and productivity of labor

General Improvement
1. Departmental layout
2. Flow of work
3. Work plan layout
4. Utilization of manpower
5. Work methods
6. Materials handling
7. Utilization of equipment
8. Motion economy

Corrective Techniques
1. Study with scale model
2. Flow chart study
3. Motion analysis
4. Comparison of units produced to standard allowance
5. Methods analysis
6. Flow chart and equipment study
7. Down time vs. running time
8. Motion analysis

M. A Planning Checklist
1. Objectives
2. Controls
3. Delegations
4. Communications
5. Resources
6. Manpower

7. Equipment
8. Supplies and materials
9. Utilization of time
10. Safety
11. Money
12. Work
13. Timing of improvements

N. Five Characteristics of Good Directions
In order to get results, directions must be:
1. Possible of accomplishment
2. Agreeable with worker interests
3. Related to mission
4. Planned and complete
5. Unmistakably clear

O. Types of Directions
1. Demands or direct orders
2. Requests
3. Suggestion or implication
4. volunteering

P. Controls
A typical listing of the overall areas in which the supervisor should establish controls might be:
1. Manpower
2. Materials
3. Quality of work
4. Quantity of work
5. Time
6. Space
7. Money
8. Methods

Q. Orienting the New Employee
1. Prepare for him
2. Welcome the new employee
3. Orientation for the job
4. Follow-up

R. Checklist for Orienting New Employees   Yes   No
1. Do you appreciate the feelings of new employees
   when they first report for work?   ___   ___
2. Are you aware of the fact that the new employee must
   make a big adjustment to his job?   ___   ___
3. Have you given him good reasons for liking the job and
   the organization?   ___   ___
4. Have you prepared for his first day on the job?   ___   ___
5. Did you welcome him cordially and make him feel needed?   ___   ___

		Yes	No
6.	Did you establish rapport with him so that he feels free to talk and discuss matters with you?	___	___
7.	Did you explain his job to him and his relationship to you?	___	___
8.	Does he know that his work will be evaluated periodically on a basis that is fair and objective?	___	___
9.	Did you introduce him to his fellow workers in such a way that they are likely to accept him?	___	___
10.	Does he know what employee benefits he will receive?	___	___
11.	Does he understand the importance of being on the job and what to do if he must leave his duty station?	___	___
12.	Has he been impressed with the importance of accident prevention and safe practice?	___	___
13.	Does he generally know his way around the department?	___	___
14.	Is he under the guidance of a sponsor who will teach the right way of doing things?	___	___
15.	Do you plan to follow-up so that he will continue to adjust successfully to his job?	___	___

S. Principles of Learning
   1. Motivation
   2. Demonstration or explanation
   3. Practice

T. Causes of Poor Performance
   1. Improper training for job
   2. Wrong tools
   3. Inadequate directions
   4. Lack of supervisory follow-up
   5. Poor communications
   6. Lack of standards of performance
   7. Wrong work habits
   8. Low morale
   9. Other

U. Four Major Steps in On-The-Job Instruction
   1. Prepare the worker
   2. Present the operation
   3. Tryout performance
   4. Follow-up

V. Employees Want Five Things
   1. Security
   2. Opportunity
   3. Recognition
   4. Inclusion
   5. Expression

W. Some Don'ts in Regard to Praise
1. Don't praise a person for something he hasn't done.
2. Don't praise a person unless you can be sincere.
3. Don't be sparing in praise just because your superior withholds it from you.
4. Don't let too much time elapse between good performance and recognition of it

X. How to Gain Your Workers' Confidence
Methods of developing confidence include such things as:
1. Knowing the interests, habits, hobbies of employees
2. Admitting your own inadequacies
3. Sharing and telling of confidence in others
4. Supporting people when they are in trouble
5. Delegating matters that can be well handled
6. Being frank and straightforward about problems and working conditions
7. Encouraging others to bring their problems to you
8. Taking action on problems which impede worker progress

Y. Sources of Employee Problems
On-the-job causes might be such things as:
1. A feeling that favoritism is exercised in assignments
2. Assignment of overtime
3. An undue amount of supervision
4. Changing methods or systems
5. Stealing of ideas or trade secrets
6. Lack of interest in job
7. Threat of reduction in force
8. Ignorance or lack of communications
9. Poor equipment
10. Lack of knowing how supervisor feels toward employee
11. Shift assignments

Off-the-job problems might have to do with:
1. Health
2. Finances
3. Housing
4. Family

Z. The Supervisor's Key to Discipline
There are several key points about discipline which the supervisor should keep in mind:
1. Job discipline is one of the disciplines of life and is directed by the supervisor.
2. It is more important to correct an employee fault than to fix blame for it.
3. Employee performance is affected by problems both on the job and off.
4. Sudden or abrupt changes in behavior can be indications of important employee problems.
5. Problems should be dealt with as soon as possible after they are identified.
6. The attitude of the supervisor may have more to do with solving problems than the techniques of problem solving.
7. Correction of employee behavior should be resorted to only after the supervisor is sure that training or counseling will not be helpful.

8. Be sure to document your disciplinary actions.
9. Make sure that you are disciplining on the basis of facts rather than personal feelings.
10. Take each disciplinary step in order, being careful not to make snap judgments, or decisions based on impatience.

AA. Five Important Processes of Management
1. Planning
2. Organizing
3. Scheduling
4. Controlling
5. Motivating

BB. When the Supervisor Fails to Plan
1. Supervisor creates impression of not knowing his job
2. May lead to excessive overtime
3. Job runs itself—supervisor lacks control
4. Deadlines and appointments missed
5. Parts of the work go undone
6. Work interrupted by emergencies
7. Sets a bad example
8. Uneven workload creates peaks and valleys
9. Too much time on minor details at expense of more important tasks

CC. Fourteen General Principles of Management
1. Division of work
2. Authority and responsibility
3. Discipline
4. Unity of command
5. Unity of direction
6. Subordination of individual interest to general interest
7. Remuneration of personnel
8. Centralization
9. Scalar chain
10. Order
11. Equity
12. Stability of tenure of personnel
13. Initiative
14. Esprit de corps

DD. Change

Bringing about change is perhaps attempted more often, and yet less well understood, than anything else the supervisor does. How do people generally react to change? (People tend to resist change that is imposed upon them by other individuals or circumstances.

Change is characteristic of every situation. It is a part of every real endeavor where the efforts of people are concerned.

1. Why do people resist change?
   People may resist change because of:
   a. Fear of the unknown
   b. Implied criticism
   c. Unpleasant experiences in the past
   d. Fear of loss of status
   e. Threat to the ego
   f. Fear of loss of economic stability

2. How can we best overcome the resistance to change?
   In initiating change, take these steps:
   a. Get ready to sell
   b. Identify sources of help
   c. Anticipate objections
   d. Sell benefits
   e. Listen in depth
   f. Follow up

II. Brief Topical Summaries

   A. Who/What is the Supervisor?
      1. The supervisor is often called the "highest level employee and the lowest level manager."
      2. A supervisor is a member of both management and the work group. He acts as a bridge between the two.
      3. Most problems in supervision are in the area of human relations, or people problems.
      4. Employees expect: Respect, opportunity to learn and to advance, and a sense of belonging, and so forth.
      5. Supervisors are responsible for directing people and organizing work. Planning is of paramount importance.
      6. A position description is a set of duties and responsibilities inherent to a given position.
      7. It is important to keep the position description up-to-date and to provide each employee with his own copy.

   B. The Sociology of Work
      1. People are alike in many ways; however, each individual is unique.
      2. The supervisor is challenged in getting to know employee differences. Acquiring skills in evaluating individuals is an asset.
      3. Maintaining meaningful working relationships in the organization is of great importance.
      4. The supervisor has an obligation to help individuals to develop to their fullest potential.
      5. Job rotation on a planned basis helps to build versatility and to maintain interest and enthusiasm in work groups.
      6. Cross training (job rotation) provides backup skills.

7. The supervisor can help reduce tension by maintaining a sense of humor, providing guidance to employees, and by making reasonable and timely decisions. Employees respond favorably to working under reasonably predictable circumstances.
8. Change is characteristic of all managerial behavior. The supervisor must adjust to changes in procedures, new methods, technological changes, and to a number of new and sometimes challenging situations.
9. To overcome the natural tendency for people to resist change, the supervisor should become more skillful in initiating change.

C. Principles and Practices of Supervision
1. Employees should be required to answer to only one superior.
2. A supervisor can effectively direct only a limited number of employees, depending upon the complexity, variety, and proximity of the jobs involved.
3. The organizational chart presents the organization in graphic form. It reflects lines of authority and responsibility as well as interrelationships of units within the organization.
4. Distribution of work can be improved through an analysis using the "Work Distribution Chart."
5. The "Work Distribution Chart" reflects the division of work within a unit in understandable form.
6. When related tasks are given to an employee, he has a better chance of increasing his skills through training.
7. The individual who is given the responsibility for tasks must also be given the appropriate authority to insure adequate results.
8. The supervisor should delegate repetitive, routine work. Preparation of recurring reports, maintaining leave and attendance records are some examples.
9. Good discipline is essential to good task performance. Discipline is reflected in the actions of employees on the job in the absence of supervision.
10. Disciplinary action may have to be taken when the positive aspects of discipline have failed. Reprimand, warning, and suspension are examples of disciplinary action.
11. If a situation calls for a reprimand, be sure it is deserved and remember it is to be done in private.

D. Dynamic Leadership
1. A style is a personal method or manner of exerting influence.
2. Authoritarian leaders often see themselves as the source of power and authority.
3. The democratic leader often perceives the group as the source of authority and power.
4. Supervisors tend to do better when using the pattern of leadership that is most natural for them.
5. Social scientists suggest that the effective supervisor use the leadership style that best fits the problem or circumstances involved.
6. All four styles—telling, selling, consulting, joining—have their place. Using one does not preclude using the other at another time.

7. The theory X point of view assumes that the average person dislikes work, will avoid it whenever possible, and must be coerced to achieve organizational objectives.
8. The theory Y point of view assumes that the average person considers work to be a natural as play, and, when the individual is committed, he requires little supervision or direction to accomplish desired objectives.
9. The leader's basic assumptions concerning human behavior and human nature affect his actions, decisions, and other managerial practices.
10. Dissatisfaction among employees is often present, but difficult to isolate. The supervisor should seek to weaken dissatisfaction by keeping promises, being sincere and considerate, keeping employees informed, and so forth.
11. Constructive suggestions should be encouraged during the natural progress of the work.

E. Processes for Solving Problems
1. People find their daily tasks more meaningful and satisfying when they can improve them.
2. The causes of problems, or the key factors, are often hidden in the background. Ability to solve problems often involves the ability to isolate them from their backgrounds. There is some substance to the cliché that some persons "can't see the forest for the trees."
3. New procedures are often developed from old ones. Problems should be broken down into manageable parts. New ideas can be adapted from old one.
4. People think differently in problem-solving situations. Using a logical, patterned approach is often useful. One approach found to be useful includes these steps:
   a. Define the problem
   b. Establish objectives
   c. Get the facts
   d. Weigh and decide
   e. Take action
   f. Evaluate action

F. Training for Results
1. Participants respond best when they feel training is important to them.
2. The supervisor has responsibility for the training and development of those who report to him.
3. When training is delegated to others, great care must be exercised to insure the trainer has knowledge, aptitude, and interest for his work as a trainer.
4. Training (learning) of some type goes on continually. The most successful supervisor makes certain the learning contributes in a productive manner to operational goals.
5. New employees are particularly susceptible to training. Older employees facing new job situations require specific training, as well as having need for development and growth opportunities.
6. Training needs require continuous monitoring.
7. The training officer of an agency is a professional with a responsibility to assist supervisors in solving training problems.

8. Many of the self-development steps important to the supervisor's own growth are equally important to the development of peers and subordinates. Knowledge of these is important when the supervisor consults with others on development and growth opportunities.

G. Health, Safety, and Accident Prevention
1. Management-minded supervisors take appropriate measures to assist employees in maintaining health and in assuring safe practices in the work environment.
2. Effective safety training and practices help to avoid injury and accidents.
3. Safety should be a management goal. All infractions of safety which are observed should be corrected without exception.
4. Employees' safety attitude, training and instruction, provision of safe tools and equipment, supervision, and leadership are considered highly important factors which contribute to safety and which can be influenced directly by supervisors.
5. When accidents do occur, they should be investigated promptly for very important reasons, including the fact that information which is gained can be used to prevent accidents in the future.

H. Equal Employment Opportunity
1. The supervisor should endeavor to treat all employees fairly, without regard to religion, race, sex, or national origin.
2. Groups tend to reflect the attitude of the leader. Prejudice can be detected even in very subtle form. Supervisors must strive to create a feeling of mutual respect and confidence in every employee.
3. Complete utilization of all human resources is a national goal. Equitable consideration should be accorded women in the work force, minority-group members, the physically and mentally handicapped, and the older employee. The important question is: "Who can do the job?"
4. Training opportunities, recognition for performance, overtime assignments, promotional opportunities, and all other personnel actions are to be handled on an equitable basis.

I. Improving Communications
1. Communications is achieving understanding between the sender and the receiver of a message. It also means sharing information—the creation of understanding.
2. Communication is basic to all human activity. Words are means of conveying meanings; however, real meanings are in people.
3. There are very practical differences in the effectiveness of one-way, impersonal, and two-way communications. Words spoken face-to-face are better understood. Telephone conversations are effective, but lack the rapport of person-to-person exchanges. The whole person communicates.
4. Cooperation and communication in an organization go hand in hand. When there is a mutual respect between people, spelling out rules and procedures for communicating is unnecessary.
5. There are several barriers to effective communications. These include failure to listen with respect and understanding, lack of skill in feedback, and misinterpreting the meanings of words used by the speaker. It is also common

practice to listen to what we want to hear, and tune out things we do not want to hear.
6. Communication is management's chief problem. The supervisor should accept the challenge to communicate more effectively and to improve interagency and intra-agency communications.
7. The supervisor may often plan for and conduct meetings. The planning phase is critical and may determine the success or the failure of a meeting.
8. Speaking before groups usually requires extra effort. Stage fright may never disappear completely, but it can be controlled.

J. Self-Development
1. Every employee is responsible for his own self-development.
2. Toastmaster and toastmistress clubs offer opportunities to improve skills in oral communications.
3. Planning for one's own self-development is of vital importance. Supervisors know their own strengths and limitations better than anyone else.
4. Many opportunities are open to aid the supervisor in his developmental efforts, including job assignments; training opportunities, both governmental and non-governmental—to include universities and professional conferences and seminars.
5. Programmed instruction offers a means of studying at one's own rate.
6. Where difficulties may arise from a supervisor's being away from his work for training, he may participate in televised home study or correspondence courses to meet his self-development needs.

K. Teaching and Training
1. The Teaching Process
Teaching is encouraging and guiding the learning activities of students toward established goals. In most cases this process consists of five steps: preparation, presentation, summarization, evaluation, and application.

   a. Preparation
   Preparation is two-fold in nature; that of the supervisor and the employee. Preparation by the supervisor is absolutely essential to success. He must know what, when, where, how, and whom he will teach. Some of the factors that should be considered are:
   1) The objectives
   2) The materials needed
   3) The methods to be used
   4) Employee participation
   5) Employee interest
   6) Training aids
   7) Evaluation
   8) Summarization

   Employee preparation consists in preparing the employee to receive the material. Probably the most important single factor in the preparation of the employee is arousing and maintaining his interest. He must know the objectives of the training, why he is there, how the material can be used, and its importance to him.

b. Presentation
   In presentation, have a carefully designed plan and follow it. The plan should be accurate and complete, yet flexible enough to meet situations as they arise. The method of presentation will be determined by the particular situation and objectives.

c. Summary
   A summary should be made at the end of every training unit and program. In addition, there may be internal summaries depending on the nature of the material being taught. The important thing is that the trainee must always be able to understand how each part of the new material relates to the whole.

d. Application
   The supervisor must arrange work so the employee will be given a chance to apply new knowledge or skills while the material is still clear in his mind and interest is high. The trainee does not really know whether he has learned the material until he has been given a chance to apply it. If the material is not applied, it loses most of its value.

e. Evaluation
   The purpose of all training is to promote learning. To determine whether the training has been a success or failure, the supervisor must evaluate this learning.
   In the broadest sense, evaluation includes all the devices, methods, skills, and techniques used by the supervisor to keep himself and the employees informed as to their progress toward the objectives they are pursuing. The extent to which the employee has mastered the knowledge, skills, and abilities, or changed his attitudes, as determined by the program objectives, is the extent to which instruction has succeeded or failed.
   Evaluation should not be confined to the end of the lesson, day, or program but should be used continuously. We shall note later the way this relates to the rest of the teaching process.

2. Teaching Methods
   A teaching method is a pattern of identifiable student and instructor activity used in presenting training material.
   All supervisors are faced with the problem of deciding which method should be used at a given time.

   a. Lecture
      The lecture is direct oral presentation of material by the supervisor. The present trend is to place less emphasis on the trainer's activity and more on that of the trainee.

   b. Discussion
      Teaching by discussion or conference involves using questions and other techniques to arouse interest and focus attention upon certain areas, and by doing so creating a learning situation. This can be one of the most

valuable methods because it gives the employees an opportunity to express their ideas and pool their knowledge.

    c. Demonstration
The demonstration is used to teach how something works or how to do something. It can be used to show a principle or what the results of a series of actions will be. A well-staged demonstration is particularly effective because it shows proper methods of performance in a realistic manner.

    d. Performance
Performance is one of the most fundamental of all learning techniques or teaching methods. The trainee may be able to tell how a specific operation should be performed but he cannot be sure he knows how to perform the operation until he has done so.
As with all methods, there are certain advantages and disadvantages to each method.

    e. Which Method to Use
Moreover, there are other methods and techniques of teaching. It is difficult to use any method without other methods entering into it. In any learning situation, a combination of methods is usually more effective than any one method alone.

Finally, evaluation must be integrated into the other aspects of the teaching-learning process.

It must be used in the motivation of the trainees; it must be used to assist in developing understanding during the training; and it must be related to employee application of the results of training.

This is distinctly the role of the supervisor.

BASIC FUNDAMENTALS OF THE MAINTENANCE OF FLOORS

CONTENTS

	Page
FLOOR TYPES	1
BUFFING TECHNIQUE	11
STRIPPING	13
FINISHING FLOORS	18
SPRAY BUFFING	20
CARPET CARE	22

BASIC FUNDAMENTALS OF THE MAINTENANCE OF FLOORS

FLOOR TYPES

I. Resilient—Elastic or Soft Floor

A. ASPHALT TILE
 1. Made from asphalt-treated asbestos fibers, with an inert filler (usually limestone) to give it hardness. For darker colored tile, gilsonite (black) asphalt is used. In lighter colors, coal tar resins are used for binders. Ingredients are mixed under heat and transferred to hot rollers, where the mix is rolled into uniform thickness.

 2. Precautions. Never use varnish, spirit waxes or solvent-type cleaners. Do not sweep asphalt tile floors with sweeping compounds containing fine oil or petroleum distillities.

B. VINYL TILE
 1. Vinyl plastic (resin) is manufactured with vinyl-resin along with color pigments and fillers. It has all the advantages of asphalt tile, plus being more flexible, and almost impervious and immune to damage by petroleum products.

C. RUBBER TILE
 1. Is generally made from synthetic, reclaimed, or pure rubber; color pigments; and inert fillers. The mix is fused and used like other rubber products, molded under pressure to required thickness, and then made into sheets of tile. It has the advantages of asphalt and vinyl floors, plus being the most pliable. It recovers from indention and resists cracking.

 2. Precautions. Oil, grease, naphtha and similar petroleum products will soften and deteriorate rubber tile. Do not sweep with sweeping compounds containing oils or petroleum distillities. Air and sunlight cause rubber tile to crack or check. Do not use shellac, varnish, lacquer, alkaline soaps, or abrasives on rubber floors.

D. LINOLEUM
 1. It is made of oxidized linseed oil, resins, and other filler material thoroughly mixed with ground cork and color pigments. The mixture is pressed out on a backing material (normally burlap) by running the mix through rollers, then curing at high temperature.

 2. Precautions. Same as asphalt tile.

E. MASTIC FLOORS
 1. Similar to asphalt tile in composition, but ingredients are heated on the job and troweled on, to form a seamless flooring material.

 2. Precautions. Same as asphalt tile.

F. CORK FLOORING
 1. Is made by compressing or baking cork curlings and ground cork, or by adding synthetic resin binders. The baking causes natural gums and resins in the cork to liquify, thus binding together the cork particles.

GENERAL POINTS TO BE OBSERVED IN MAINTENANCE OF ALL RESILIENT FLOORING:

1. All resilient flooring material should be cleaned and a floor finish applied (either wax or

synthetic) as soon as floor has been allowed to set up. These floors should be cleaned and a finish applied on regular schedule, throughout the life of the floor.

2. Being a semi-soft material, it should be kept free of sand and dirt, which may scratch or discolor the surface.

3. Thorough dusting with a properly treated dust mop is important. To reduce the number of scrubbings necessary, oil and solvent type dust mop treatment should not be used. Damp or wet mopping should be utilized to remove surface soil conditions (mud, water and sand).

4. Spray buffing in heavy traffic areas will maintain these areas looking as well as non-traffic areas. It lengthens the time between stripping. Remember that spray buffing is not a cure for all maintenance problems.

5. Buffing is an absolute necessity in areas where traffic is heavy.

6. The legs of chairs, tables, and desks should be equipped with coasters or glides to prevent denting or marking of floor.

II. Hard Floors

A. CONCRETE

1. Concrete floors are mixtures of cement with varying proportions of sand and gravel. The porosity and smoothness of the surface depends upon the mix and the hardening and finishing process. Color pigments are often added to the topping mix when concrete is used as a decorative floor material.

2. Maintenance for Concrete Floors:

a. Concrete floors protected by concrete sealer and wax will require only dust mopping or floor brushing to keep them clean and attractive. Concrete floors may be cleaned with any mild cleaning solution; however, care should be taken in proper rinsing.

b. If a concrete floor dusts excessively, it should be scrubbed with a neutral soap and sealed. Proper sealing will greatly lengthen concrete floor life, prevent dusting, and make maintenance easier and more economical. When traffic lanes begin to show, the floor can easily be touched up. Properly done, this treatment will not show an overlap.

c. Concrete floors can be waxed rather than sealed. However, better results will be achieved by sealing the floor and then applying a coat of wax. After this treatment, periodic buffing, using a fine nylon disc, will greatly reduce maintenance time, and decrease the frequency of stripping and refinishing.

B. TERRAZZO

1. Terrazzo is one of the oldest flooring materials. It was used in pre-Christian times in many palaces and mansions of ancient rulers and merchants.

2. It is a hard, durable composition material, made up of marble chips and cement matrix. This surface, after hardening for a time, is wet ground under pressure with stone grinders. Because of its pattern, terrazzo does not readily show soil and stays presentable longer than floors of one color.

3. Special Precautions in Maintenance of Terrazzo:

MAINTENANCE OF FLOORS

a. Cleaning materials containing acids or alkalines should be avoided, since the acid or alkali eats into the cement and loosens the marble chips.

b. Avoid abrasive powder cleaners because they encourage "dusting." This type of cleaner actually wears away the floor, and its ill effects are noticeable within a short period of time.

c. Cleaning crystals of a phosphate nature should never be used. A residue remains after the water has evaporated and acts in much the same way as water when it is allowed to stand in a concrete formation and is then frozen. In other words, the crystals fill up porous spots in the cement; and as they dry, they expand. The expansion loosens the marble chips; this is called "spalling."

d. Avoid sweeping compounds containing oil. These will penetrate and discolor terrazzo.

4. Maintenance for Terrazzo Floors

a. In scrubbing a terrazzo floor, do not use steel wool. It is best to use a brush for scrubbing because the steel wool is softer than the terrazzo and may become abraded. Bits of the wool left on the floor will rust and stain the terrazzo. Also, the use of steel wool on terrazzo can result in black carbon marks. Clean terrazzo with neutral, synthetic, free-rinsing liquid detergent. These detergents will leave no unsightly residue that often necessitates special work and materials to remove it.

b. Terrazzo floors should be mopped frequently and rinsed thoroughly. Dirty water will stain if left too long; it leaves a gummy hardened accumulation of film which is not easily removed.

c. The use of a solvent type "water white" sealer on terrazzo will prevent dusting and spalling. However, a heavy surface film of this material allowed to build up will result in severe traffic laning. Color variations in the floor may also appear.

d. Properly applied, colorless, buffable-type terrazzo seal, well-rubbed out, tends to harden the surface, helps hold the marble chips together, and virtually stops penetration of water, stains, oils, gums and other damaging materials. The finish will have a satin-like sheen.

e. Either solvent or water emulsion-type wax can be used on terrazzo. However, only waxes manufacured from light colored products should be used. Solvent-type wax manufactured from waxed having a very dark color, or solvent waxes to which artificial coloring matter has been added, would definitely cause a discoloration of terrazzo. Serious discoloration could also occur if a water wax emulsion made from dark colored waxes is applied to a terrazzo floor.

C. MARBLE

1. Marble is a natural product of crystallized rock, composed of carbonate of lime. Generally, marble used in the interior of buildings for decorative purposes is of the polished, finished type which reflects light because of its glossy surface. This also emphasizes color and marking. Marble used for interior floors may have a "honed" or a "sand" finish.

a. Travertine marble, recognized by its small pits and tarnish-colored surface, requires only cleaning, as does polished marble. Travertine is used generally as wainscot or other trim material.

2. On all types of marble, except the Travertine, sealing is recommended. The primary purpose of this treatment is to provide maximum protection to the marble itself, which is very soft and porous. Ordinary dirt and grease are sealed out of the floor, and because the pits and voids have been filled, the soil is held on the surface and is easy to remove through usual maintenance methods.

3. Marble floors sealed and finished with a good, colorless, buffable type terrazzo sealer can be maintained dry with only occasional mopping. Sealers of solvent cut resin or lacquer nature, used on marble floors, result in traffic laning, uneven appearance of the floor surface, and over a period of time, discoloration of the surface.

4. Special Precautions in Maintenance of Marble:

a. Never use an acid cleaner. It will destroy polish and eventually burn. The end result will be discoloration and disintegration of the marble.

b. Do not use scouring bricks or harsh abrasives. These materials will destroy polish and mar the surface.

c. Bar, powder, or liquid soaps should not be used on marble surfaces. They may form insoluble deposits which accumulate on the surface. This discoloration cannot be readily removed and will become a slip hazard when wet.

d. Never use oily sweeping compounds on marble surfaces. Their use will eventually discolor the floor.

e. Quick action "lightening" cleaners are apt to be acid in action. The life and finish of the marble will be sacrificed for immediate results.

5. Maintenance for Marble Floors:

a. The secret to beautiful marble is merely keeping it clean after the original sealing treatment. Complicated cleaning agents and procedures will rarely be needed if the marble surfaces are maintained properly and regularly. When complete cleaning is necessary, use a neutral, free-rinsing detergent that will not leave a slippery or unattractive residue.

b. Marble spalling and deterioration can be caused through neglect. Marble is not indestructable, and when neglected, the accumulated dirt and grease can completely deteriorate and damage the surface beyond repair.

D. OXYCHLORIDE

1. Oxychloride, sometimes called magnasite, is similar to concrete. It is produced in many colors. It can be installed with two types of finish. One type of finish is trowelled on. The other type of finish is ground and gives the appearance of being terrazzo. It can be laid over nearly any type of sub-floor and produces a surface which is rather resilient, yet dense and strong. However, magnasite is a somewhat porous and soft material as compared to terrazzo or concrete.

2. Special Precautions in Maintenance of Oxychloride:

a. Avoid use of strong alkalies for cleaning.

b. Acids used in some cleaning materials tend to dissolve oxychloride due to chemical reaction and should not be used.

MAINTENANCE OF FLOORS

c. Avoid excessive use of water. This material is ever-thirsty, and deterioration of the binder will result.

3. Maintenance for Oxychloride Floors:

a. In cleaning, a neutral soap or a non-alkaline detergent should be used. The application procedure is listed under asphalt tile.

b. Oxychloride flooring is porous and may be sealed with a penetrating-type sealer. Sealing will fill the pores of the floor covering, and maintenance work will become easier.

c. When excessively soiled, oxychloride floors should be scrubbed with a floor machine, using a scrubbing brush. However, the excessive use of water will damage some of the fillers, and will also attack the magnesium oxychloride binder and deteriorate it. For this reason, oxychloride floors should be sealed and waxed.

d. Solvent-type wax should be used on this flooring. Oily floor dressings should not be used as they could result in serious discoloration. Sweeping compounds containing organic dyes and free oil could also cause discoloration, and any sand present in the compound could result in the scratching and abrading of the rather soft oxychloride floor.

E. HARD TILE

1. Ceramic tile or "hard tile" is made of finely ground clay and baked to the hardness of stone. The various types include ceramic mosaic, quarry, and clear glaze.

2. Hard tile is naturally durable and resistant to soil defacement; but to get full value from a large investment, it has to have the same care as more susceptible flooring materials. Hard tile can be either glazed or unglazed. Tile used as flooring material is usually unglazed. Glazed tile is normally used as wall surfacings.

3. Special Precautions in Maintenance of Hard Tile:

a. Avoid solutions of strong alkaline cleaners, such as tri-sodium phosphate and sal soda. These cleaners penetrate the cement grout between the tile and upon drying, leave crystallized deposits. Continued use of alkaline cleaners will cause the crystallized deposits to accumulate and swell, causing disintegration of the grout.

b. Do not use steel wool for cleaning hard tile. The tile is harder than the steel wool and will abrade the wool, causing discoloration of the tile. Abrasive cleansers should never be used on the glazed surfaces.

c. Do not use acid cleaners, not because they will injure the tile, but because they will tend to destroy the cement grout. They may also dull glazed or ceramic tile.

d. Oily dust mops and sweeping compounds should not be used for maintenance of hard tile floors.

4. Maintenance for Hard Tile Floors:

a. About the only maintenance process for glazed tile floors consists of dusting and spot washing. Non-alkaline synthetic cleaners are recommended for cleaning.

b. Tile used as a flooring material resists most traffic stains, but it can suffer from the erosive action of abrasion. This means not only the wear and tear from traffic; but also from abrasive cleansers, which in time, will scratch or dull the finish.

c. A penetrating sealer, such as the type used for terrazzo, will prove to be a protection for the surface and will also protect cement grout from undue deterioration. Surface sealers which leave a heavy film of a non-buffable nature should not be used.

d. Waxing a hard tile floor is not recommended because wax may become a safety hazard. Where safety is not a factor, either the water emulsion or solvent wax can be used.

F. WOOD

1. The use of hard wood floors is as old as civilization. Their durability has been an important factor in their wide use. Wood floors, properly maintained, are capable of retaining their natural good looks for a long period of time. Wood can last a lifetime and longer.

2. Special Precautions in Maintenance of Wood:

a. Use a minimum amount of water to maintain wood floors. Excessive water may enter through the ends of the wood and cause swelling or warping.

b. When wood floors are set in mastic, exercise extreme care in the use of sealers, spirit waxes, solvent cleaners, and water.

c. Select and use a maintenance method which eliminates or minimizes the necessity for resanding.

3. Maintenance for Wood Floors:

a. Any good soap, except those strongly alkaline, can be used for cleaning wood floors. However, scrubbing, or even wet mopping will ultimately damage a wood floor.

b. It is most important to understand the adverse effects of water, oil, and alkali soaps on wood. Water raises the grain on wood floors, causes swelling and warping, and in general, creates a rough surface that is difficult to maintain. Where wood floors are bonded to a sub-floor, penetrating water will weaken the bond and cause loosening. In addition, water discolors wood, gives it a musty odor, and causes it to rot. Oil softens wood, darkens it, and creates a sticky surface that picks up and holds dirt. Alkali cleaners can stain and darken wood floors.

c. Wood floors of any type require positive sealing. Seals, manufactured specifically for wood floor application, protect against penetration of moisture, and properly formulated, are resistant to acids, alkalies, and oils.

d. The two general classifications of wood sealers are called surface seal and penetrating seal. The type used depends upon the floor usage.

e. Surface sealers are used for floors which are not subjected to heavy traffic. This type forms a perceptible film on top of the wood while penetrating it to a certain extent, and sealing. The surface seals are preferred for the sake of appearance.

f. The true penetrating sealers protect the wood surface by filling the pores but leave little actual surface. The penetrating seal is better for areas of heavy traffic since its "stain" finish is less subject to marking.

g. Traffic lanes, which show up in time, can be resealed without treating the entire area. The worn areas need only be scrubbed and given a light coating. If sufficient care is used in doing the patching, the former worn spots will not be noticeable.

MAINTENANCE OF FLOORS

h. Waxing, after the seal application, is an ideal treatment to provide maximum appearance and protection. Use of a solvent-type wax is highly recommended. It will prolong the life of the wood surface by reducing the need for mopping.

STAIN REMOVAL FOR RESILIENT FLOORS

A properly maintained resilient floor covering should have sufficient wax or floor finish on the surface to protect it against most water based stains, and many oil- and solvent-based stains. Freshly spilled stains should be wiped up or blotted immediately before they have a chance to dry. Dried stains, being more difficult to remove and usually of questionable origin, may require more than one treatment of different stain removers. Never use a solvent-type cleaner (turpentine, naphtha, dry-cleaning solution) on asphalt or rubber.

GENERAL POINTS TO OBSERVE:

1. Act promptly in treating stains or spots. Stains or spots are most easily removed when fresh. Use the mildest treatment, first. Maybe blotting paper or cold water sponging will remove the stain.

2. Before treatment of the stain, wet the area around it with clear water. This tends to stop the spread of the cleaner. Always work from the outside toward the center to prevent leaving a cleaning ring.

3. Several applications may be necessary before the stain can be completely removed.

4. Water is considered a good solvent. When possible its use is recommended first. In any case, it is always best to use the simplest procedure.

5. It is important to know the surface to be treated and the nature of the stain before trying to remove the stain. If you do not know, leave it alone. Call in an expert.

    a. Is the stain water-borne? If so, water will remove it.

    b. Is the stain alcohol-borne (for example, iodine)? If so, alcohol will remove it.

    c. Is the stain alkali? Then use an acid to neutralize it.

    d. Is the stain acid? If so, use alkali.

MAINTENANCE OF FLOORS

TYPE OF STAIN	TREATMENT
Acids	Clean with diluted general purpose cleaner. Strong acids may require neutralization with ammonia solution.
Adhesives, Flooring	Rub with nylon pad dipped in dilute cleaner. Some mastic adhesives may respond better to concentrated cleaner and nylon pad. Use alcohol on asphalt or rubber.
Alcoholic Beverages	Rub with nylon pad dipped in dilute cleaner. Wine stains might require alcohol or hydrogen peroxide.
Alkalies	Neutralize with acetic acid 5% solution (vinegar), rinse thoroughly, dry and apply polish.
Blood	First, the soiled area should be washed with plain, clear, cold water. Then, a few drops of ammonia should be applied to the area.
Candle Wax	Scrape off with putty knife. Wash with dilute cleaner, rinse, dry and apply polish. Use concentrated cleaner for asphalt and rubber.
Candy	Scrape off with putty knife. Apply diluted cleaner, rub with nylon pad.
Chewing Gum	Scrape off with putty knife. Scraping may be more effective if gum is first frozen with dry ice. Wash with diluted cleaner, rinse, dry and apply polish. Use concentrated cleaner for asphalt and rubber.
Chocolate	Scrape off with putty knife. Rub with nylon pad dipped in dilute cleaner. Rinse, dry and apply polish if necessary.
Cigarette Burns	Rub with coarse, then mild, nylon pad dipped in dilute cleaner. Rinse and dry. Slight indentations may require patching.

MAINTENANCE OF FLOORS

Coffee	Wash with diluted cleaner. A build-up of residue may require the use of mild nylon pad. If stain is old, place over it an absorbent cloth saturated with a glycerin solution. Let stand for about a half hour. Then, reclean with dilute cleaner. A deep stain may require the use of hydrogen peroxide.
Crayon	Scrape off with putty knife. Rub residual mark with nylon pad dipped in solution. Wash with dilute cleaner, rinse, dry and apply polish if necessary. Use concentrated cleaner for asphalt and rubber.
Fruit Juices	Use dilute cleaner. Persistent stains may require hydrogen peroxide.
Grass Stains	See Coffee
Ink, Ball Point	Clean with naphtha and/or alcohol (for asphalt and rubber, rub with nylon pad dipped in concentrated cleaner). Rinse, dry and spot polish.
Ink, Washable	Use diluted cleaner. If ink is soaked into floor, apply an alcohol-soaked blotter for several minutes. Wash with dilute cleaner, rinse, dry and apply polish.
Iodine	Clean with alcohol or an ammonia-saturated cloth. Deep stains may require longer contact with ammonia-saturated cotton. Rinse with dilute cleaner, clear water, dry and apply polish.
Lipstick	Scrape with putty knife. Rub residual stain with nylon pad dipped in concentrated cleaner. Deep stains may require the use of hydrogen peroxide followed by dilute cleaner. Rinse, dry and apply polish if necessary.
Nail Polish	Clean with acetone (use alcohol and nylon pad on asphalt and rubber).
Oil and Grease	Use diluted cleaner, rinse and dry.

MAINTENANCE OF FLOORS

For Persistent Stains

Cover stain with cotton batting soaked in hydrogen peroxide. On top of this, lay cotton batting soaked in ammonia. Repeat treatment as necessary until stain is removed.

Paint .... Use paint remover sparingly. (Do not use solvent on asphalt and rubber. Rub with nylon pad.) Apply diluted cleaner, rinse, dry and polish.

Black Rubber Marks .... Rub with nylon stripping pad dipped in concentrated cleaner. Apply dilute cleaner, rinse, dry and polish. For wood or other non-resilient floors, rub with pad dipped in cleaner or naphtha.

Rust .... Use oxalic acid solution, rinse thoroughly, dry and apply polish if necessary.

Shellac .... Clean with alcohol. Apply diluted cleaner, rinse, dry and polish.

Shoe Polish .... Rub with nylon pad dipped in concentrated cleaner. Apply dilute cleaner, rinse, dry and polish.

Solvents .... Solvents may roughen floor or cause color mixing. Burnish with an abrasive pad or nylon pad. Apply floor polish.

Tar .... See Chewing Gum.

Tobacco .... Apply diluted cleaner. On porous floors use lemon juice and water or equal parts of alcohol and glycerin. It may be necessary to bleach the stain with hydrogen peroxide or a liquid bleach.

Urine .... Apply diluted cleaning solution. If stain is old, use oxalic acid solution followed by cleaner. Rinse, dry and polish if necessary.

MAINTENANCE OF FLOORS

BUFFING TECHNIQUE

PURPOSE: To remove surface soil and renew the protective surface coating.

EQUIPMENT:

    Electric floor machine
    Nylon pads
    Treated cloths
    Brush or Drive assembly
    Sweeping tool, or
    Broom and broom bags

SAFETY PRECAUTIONS:

1. Do not leave machine unattended and plugged in.

2. Handle the machine carefully. Keep both hands on machine.

3. Always remove all cord off hooks and handle before beginning the buffing operation.

4. Check cord and plug for breaks and loose connections.

PROCEDURE

1. Assemble equipment. Take to assigned area.

2. Dust/sweep floors.

3. Tilt machine back on wheels and handle.

4. Straddle handle. Secure brush or drive assembly to drum of machine. Turn counterclockwise to lock.

5. Plug machine into most convenient outlet.

6. Stand machine on brush.

7. Adjust handle to proper height for comfort and ease of handling.

8. Raise wheels.

MAINTENANCE OF FLOORS

PROCEDURE

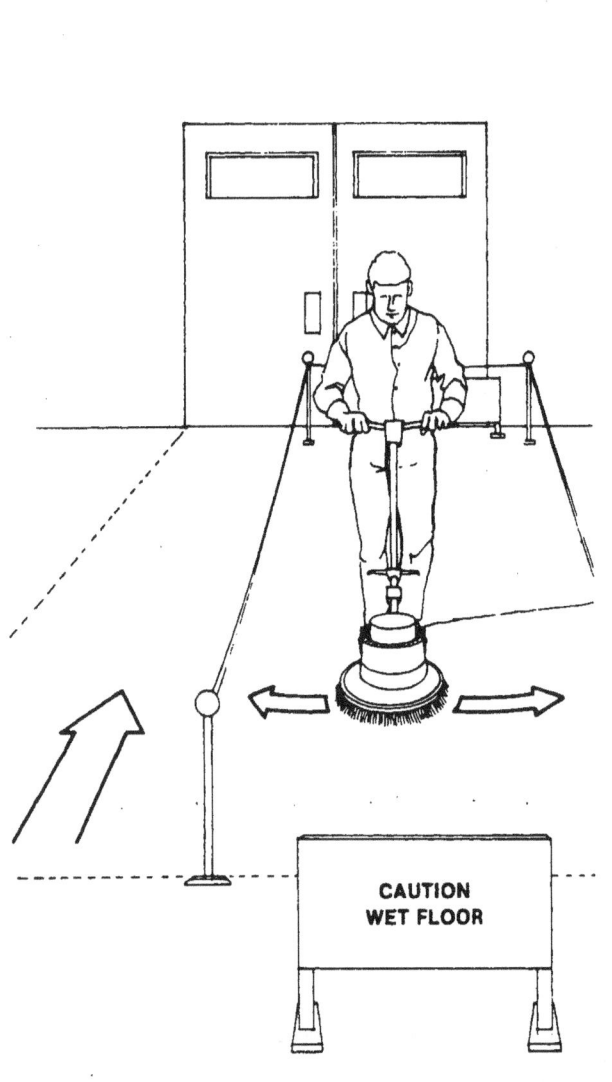

9. Begin buffing:
   a. Place cord over shoulder to keep out of path of machine. Start machine directly in front of the operator.

   b. Press downward on handle to move machine to right.

   c. Raise the handle to move the machine to the left.

   d. Move machine slowly in a left to right and right to left, or side to side arc pattern.

   e. Walk backward which facilitates easier movement of machine. However, it is safer to move forward.

10. Continue this procedure until area is completed.

11. Take equipment to utility room. Remove brush or drive assembly and pads, and wash. Wipe machine and cord off. Return to designated area.

MAINTENANCE OF FLOORS

STRIPPING
(Wet and Dry)

PURPOSE: To remove finish and embedded dirt, and to prepare floor for refinishing. This operation is performed by a combination of chemical action of the cleaning agent and the action of the brush or pad attached to an electric floor machine.

EQUIPMENT:

    Utility cart
    Nylon stripping pads
    Buckets and wringers on dolly (two)
    Mopheads and handles (two)
    Putty knife (long handle)
    Vacuum cleaner (wet and dry)
    Cloths
    Wet floor signs
    Sweeping tool—treated cloths, or
    Broom—broom bags
    Coving brush and handle
    Electric floor machine and attachments
    Drive assembly
    Scrubbing brush with pad holder
    Stripping agent
    Gloves
    Dustpan and Counter brush

SAFETY PRECAUTIONS:

1. Strip floor only on the advice of the supervisor.

2. Always sweep (use sweeping tool or covered broom) or vacuum before stripping.

3. Post area with wet floor signs.

4. Strip a small section (approximately six feet) at a time to avoid standing in solution.

5. Do not use an extension cord that is smaller than cord on machine.

6. Make sure that electric cord is free of any breaks and that the plug and outlets are grounded. Do not remove grounding prong.

7. Authorities state that adapters should not be used on portable electrical commercial equipment.

8. Place electric cord over shoulder to prevent it from becoming entangled in the machine. Hold a loop of the cord in hand so that a sudden motion will not jerk the cord and break wires.

PROCEDURE

Wet

1. Assemble equipment. Prepare solution. Take to designated area.

2. Put area out of order. Post wet floor signs.

3. Move furniture and disconnect all electrical appliances and equipment.

4. Vacuum or dust area with sweeping tool or covered broom. Remove debris with dustpan and counter brush.

MAINTENANCE OF FLOORS

PROCEDURE

5. Scrub baseboards. Use coving brush, baseboard cleaning attachment, or improvised nylon pad on mop handle to remove built-up soil from baseboards in areas where applicable.

6. Apply stripping solution to floor surface with mop. Allow to stand for two to three minutes.

7. Begin scrubbing far enough from walls to prevent the splashing of soil and solution.

8. Carry solution on floor with motion of the machine. Move slowly, but continuously—using a side-to-side, overlapping, arc pattern. Cover a six-foot path. If floors are pitted or dented, scrub in a criss-cross pattern. Turn machine slightly on edge, either to the right or left, (heeling) to remove "hard to remove" marks.

9. Pick up soil and solution. Use mop or wet vacuum. In extremely soiled areas, it may be necessary to repeat the above procedures.

10. Rinse floor and baseboards. Apply enough rinse water to completely remove all soil and solution.

11. Pick up rinse water with mop or wet vacuum.

12. Re-rinse floor surface with clear water several times in order to free surface of detergent. This is important because detergent harms some types of floor surfacing.

13. Continue entire procedure until area is completed.

14. Take equipment to utility room. Wash and dry. Wash off machines, cords, brushes, and pads. Return all equipment to designated stor-

MAINTENANCE OF FLOORS

PROCEDURE

---

age area. Restock utility cart. Place mopheads in plastic liner/bag and place in laundry bag; then store in designated area to be picked up and laundered.

- - - - - - - - - - - - - - - - -

Dry

This procedure at Saint Elizabeths Hospital is performed in restricted areas only and should be used only upon the direction of the supervisor.

ADDITIONAL EQUIPMENT:

Nylon stripping pad (coarse, aggressive, loosely woven)

Aerosol dry stripping agent

Spray attachment unit

- - - - - - - - - - - - - - - - -

SAFETY PRECAUTIONS:

1. Do not discard aerosol cans with regular trash.

PROCEDURE:

1. Assemble equipment. Attach spray unit to floor machine. Prepare mopping solution.

2. Prepare area—move furniture, unplug electric appliances and equipment.

3. Sweep or dust floor with covered broom or floor tool. Pick up debris and discard.

PROCEDURE

4. Dip mop into cleaning solution. Wring out thoroughly.

5. Damp mop area.

6. Shake aerosol stripping agent.

7. Snap can into spray unit. Keep dot on valve rim pointed down.

8. Apply stripping agent to floor (only enough for complete pad spread).
    a. Move machine *forward* and spread foam on first pass.

    b. Slowly move machine back over the same area to strip on second pass.

    c. Slowly move machine back over same area to burnish dry on third pass.

    d. Slowly move machine over same area on the fourth pass, applying stripping agent to new area—completing the four-step operation of the dry stripping system. (If the area is not dry on fourth pass, too much stripping agent was used.)

9. Move forward into next area. Overlap previous strokes and continue the four-step operation of spreading, stripping, and burnishing until area is completed.

10. Dust floor. Use *untreated* covered broom or floor tool. Pick up soil.

11. Dip mop into rinse water. Wring out thoroughly.

12. Damp mop area.

13. Apply floor finish as normally required.

MAINTENANCE OF FLOORS 17

PROCEDURE

14. Wash nylon pad immediately. Wash and dry all equipment and return to designated storage area.

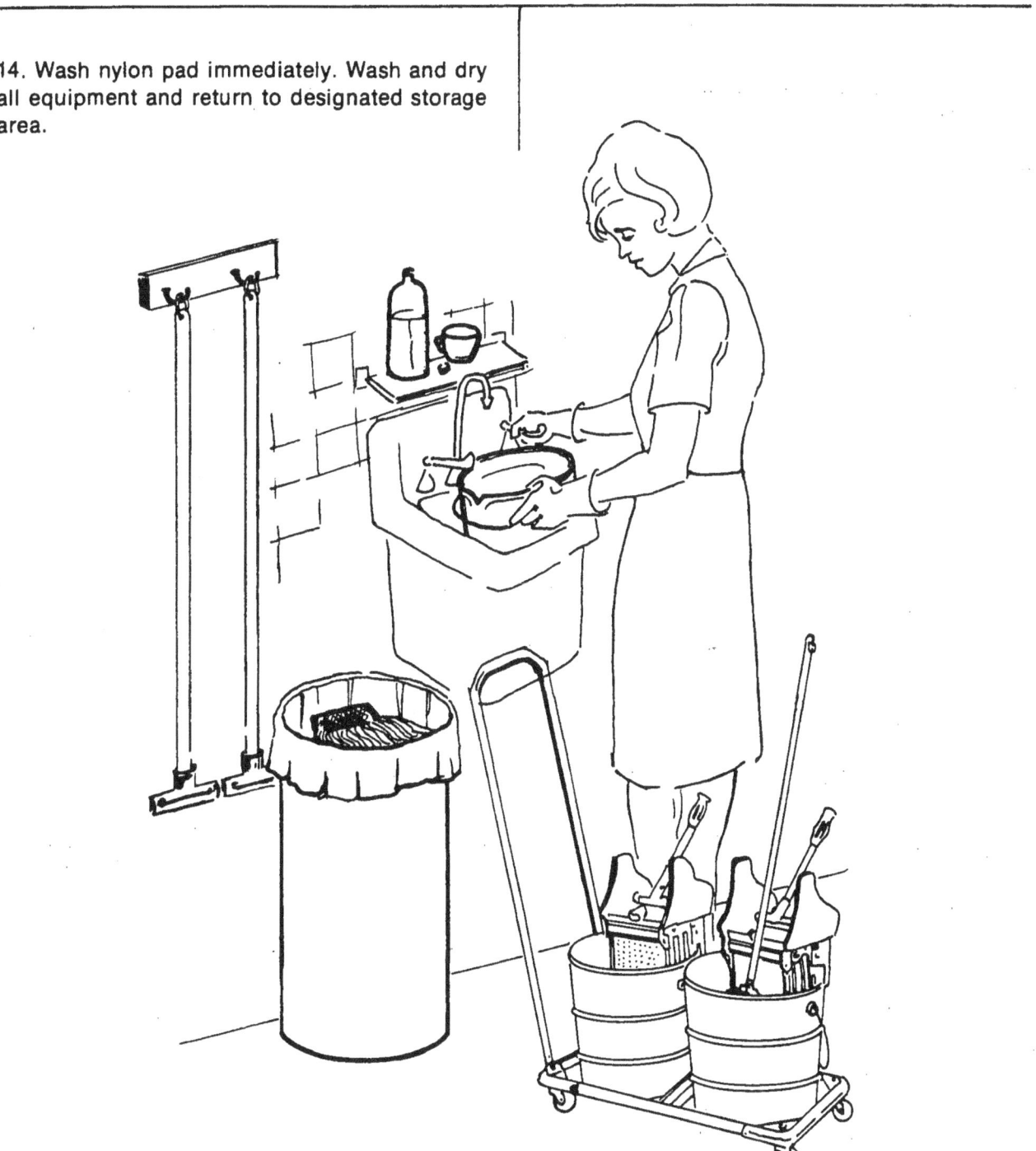

FINISHING FLOORS
(Sealers and Floor Finishes)

PURPOSE: To fill pores and cracks, prevent stains and deterioration, to provide protective coating and leveling to surface, to reduce maintenance, and to restore floors to their original finish.

EQUIPMENT:

Synthetic sealer
Synthetic Finish
Electric floor machine
Plastic liners
Buckets and Wringers on dolly (two)
Mopheads and handles (two)
Cloths

SAFETY PRECAUTIONS:

1. Do not save contaminated/soiled solution. Discard.

2. Never pour any part of the used solution back into the container.

3. Never pour or drip finish on floor.

4. Remove spills and splashes of sealer or finish immediately. If allowed to dry, will not be able to remove.

PROCEDURE

1. Assemble equipment. Place plastic liners in buckets. Fold over rim and under handle. Take to assigned area.

2. Place mophead into one bucket. Pour sealer on mophead. Wring out mophead. Continue pouring small amounts of sealer onto mophead and wringing out until mophead is saturated. (This eliminates the waste of product.) Wring out. (Make sure mop does not drip.)

3. Apply two thin coats of sealer to floor surface. Apply first coat crosswise, and apply second coat lengthwise for complete coverage. Allow time for complete drying between coats.

4. Place second mophead into second bucket. Pour floor finish on mophead. Wring out mophead. Continue pouring small amounts of finish

MAINTENANCE OF FLOORS

PROCEDURE

---

onto mophead and wringing out until mophead is saturated. Wring out.

5. Apply three thin coats of floor finish to surface. Apply first coat crosswise, second coat lengthwise, and third coat crosswise for complete coverage and surface leveling. Whenver mop pulls or drags during application, return to solution. Allow time for complete drying between coats.

6. To make surface very hard and level/smooth, buff with polishing pad after each application, or complete the procedure, and buff floor after one hour drying time. (Do not use brush—will remove finish.)

BE CERTAIN THAT YOU:

Take equipment to utility room. Wash thoroughly. Place mophead into plastic liner/bag and place in laundry bag. Return equipment to designated storage area.

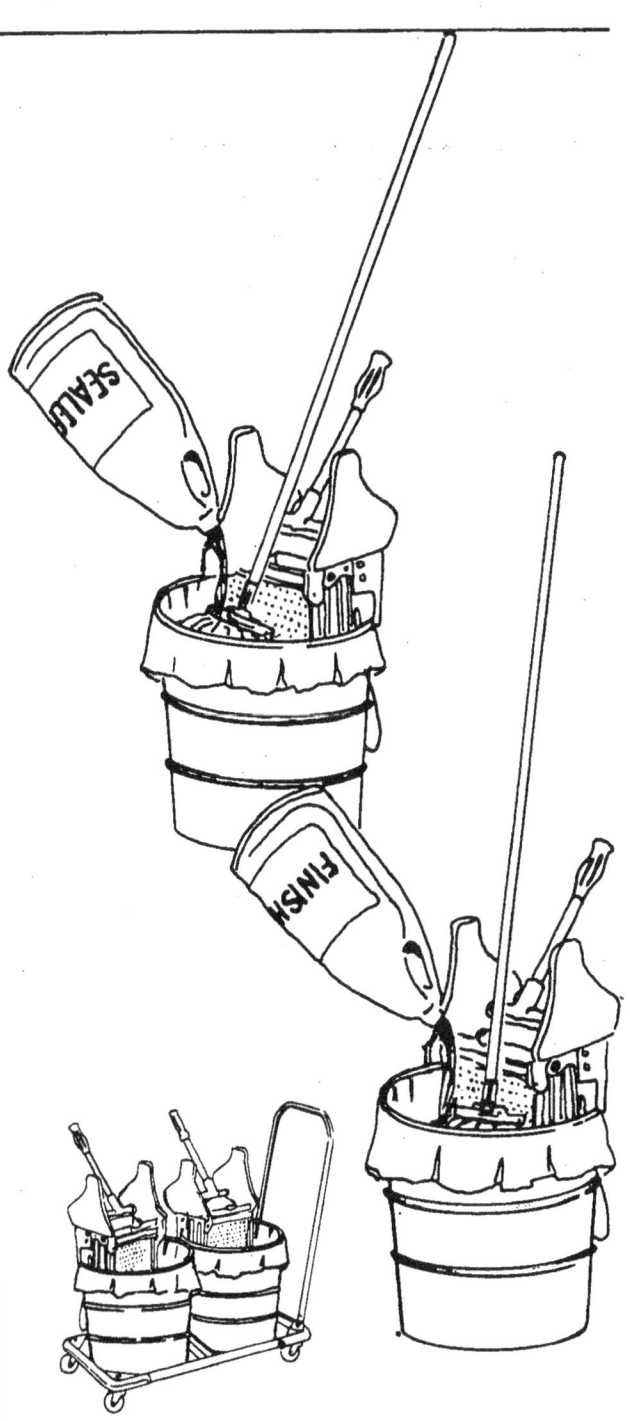

SPRAY BUFFING

PURPOSE: To maintain floor to optimum level. Also good for patching floors before they reach the point of needing a major refinishing job. Spray buffing is the basic method for maintaining resilient floors.

EQUIPMENT:

    Electric floor machine
    Aerosol cleaning agent, or
    Synthetic floor finish
    Nylon Pads (thick, loosely woven, aggressive)
    Sweeping tool
    Spray attachment unit, or
    Hand spray
    Brush with pad holder attachment, or
    Driving pad assembly
    Dustpan and Counter brush

SAFETY PRECAUTIONS:

    Same as for general buffing.

PROCEDURE

1. Assemble equipment. Attach spray unit to floor machine. Take to designated area.

2. Move furniture.

3. Sweep floor with covered floor tool. Pick up soil.

4. Shake aerosol cleaning agent. Snap can into spray unit.

5. Move floor machine to area, begin buffing as usual.

6. When black marks, spots, soil scuffs or scratches appear in the path of the buffer, spray a light mist on the areas. (If spray bottle is used, spray finish upward into air so that it falls to the floor in a mist instead of a stream.)

7. Buff same area until soil/damage is removed and shine appears. The machine will move

MAINTENANCE OF FLOORS

PROCEDURE

freely at first, then the area will become tacky or sticky before the shine appears.

8. Continue this procedure until area is repaired/clean. If area is too damaged, light scrub the area and apply thin coats of finish.

9. Remove pad or brush. Place in plastic liner. This procedure keeps pads/brushes moisted and makes cleaning easier.

10. Take equipment to utility room. Wash pads and place on flat surface or hang on peg to dry. Wipe off equipment and return to designated storage area.

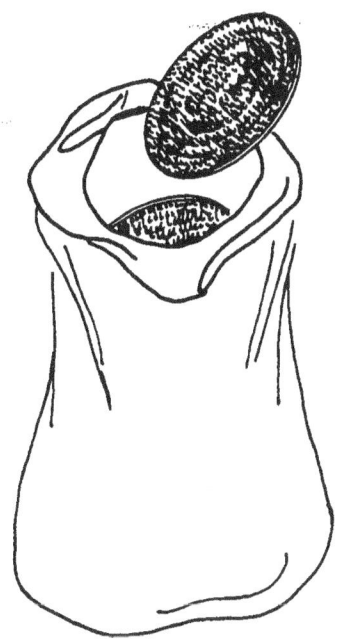

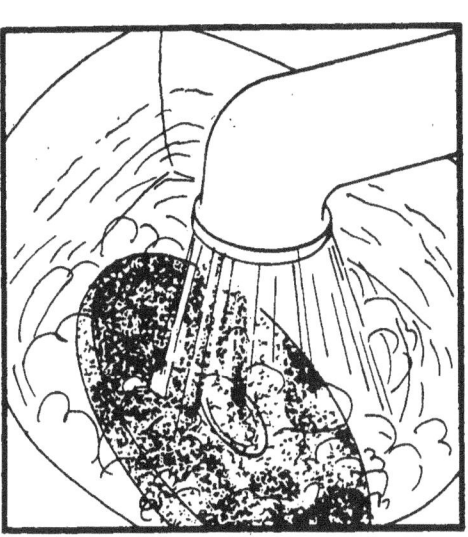

CARPET CARE
Cleaning and Spot Removal

PURPOSE: To remove dust, dirt, and grit particles, control bacteria, extend the life of the carpet and for appearance.

EQUIPMENT:

    Suction vacuum cleaner (Pile-lifting, upright machine with a brush and beater bar)
    White nylon hand brush with handle
    Shampooing machine
    Bucket and funnel
    Plastic boots or liners
    Wet and dry vacuum cleaner
    Shampooing agent
    Spot removing kit

SAFETY PRECAUTIONS:

1. Damp floors and uncleaned spills cause rot and mildew. Therefore, avoid soaking the carpet.

2. The steps to carpet care are:

    a. Vacuum

    b. Shampoo

    c. Remove spot

    d. Vacuum. Do not take any short cuts.

3. Release pressure in solution tank before removing cap.

4. Never wear shoes with dyed soles.

5. Protect carpet from rust stains. Use aluminum foil, cardboard, or plastic furniture coasters under legs of furniture.

PROCEDURE

1. Assemble equipment. Prepare solution. Pour into shampoo tank. Replace cap. Take to assigned area.

2. Move furniture. (If furniture cannot be moved out of area, move furniture to center of room. Vacuum, shampoo, remove spots, and vacuum perimeter. Replace furniture. Clean center of area/room.)

3. Vacuum with upright heavy duty pile lifting machine. Use three straight back-and-forth motions over the same area. (To prepare carpet for shampooing with regular vacuum, six back-and-forth strokes are required.)

MAINTENANCE OF FLOORS 23

PROCEDURE

4. Continue this procedure until entire carpet is vacuumed.

5. Shampoo carpet. Start in far corner of the room and work toward door. Set pile selector. Build up foam, and wait until foam appears around head of shampooing machine.

6. Take hand brush and shampoo along wall edges and corners.

7. Move machine in a forward and backward, or push and pull motion. Work across carpet, overlap each stroke.

8. Drop down to next area—overlap previous area. Continue procedure until carpet is completed.

9. If foam is brownish, vacuum immediately with wet vacuum; repeat shampooing procedure.

10. Remove any remaining spots.

11. Allow to dry.

12. Vacuuming *is a must in order to remove soil.*

13. Raise the pile with brush or machine.

14. Replace furniture. Aluminum foil, cardboard, or plastic furniture coasters may be placed under legs of furniture to avoid rust stains.

15. Take equipment to utility room. Clean. Hose off brush, wheels, and underneath shampoo machine. Wipe off exterior cabinet, and dry. Empty wet and dry vacuum. Wash and dry. Wash brush. Return all equipment to designated storage area.

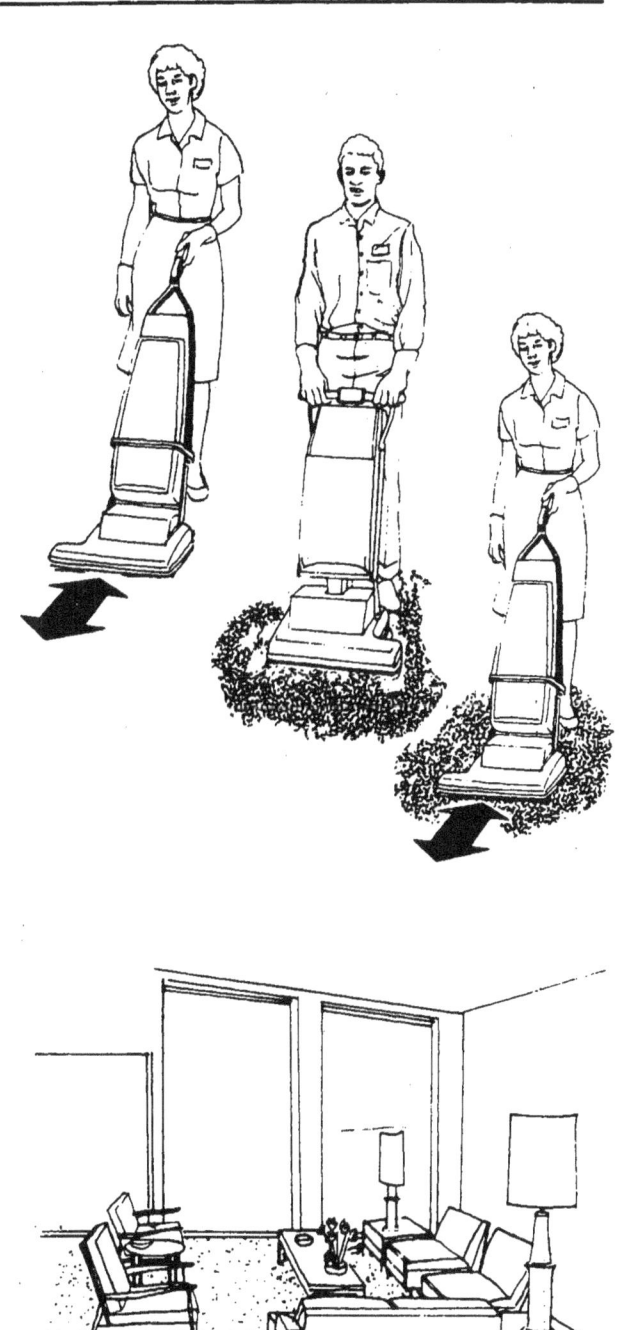

www.ingramcontent.com/pod-product-compliance
Lightning Source LLC
Chambersburg PA
CBHW081816300426
44116CB00014B/2379